Mike Pearsall

TWEETSIE COUNTRY

Mike Pearsall

TWEETSIE COUNTRY

The East Tennessee & Western North Carolina Railroad

MALLORY HOPE FERRELL

WITH ILLUSTRATIONS BY
Mike Pearsall & Casey Holtzinger

The Overmountain Press
JOHNSON CITY, TENNESSEE

Other Books By Mallory Hope Ferrell

Rails, Sagebrush & Pine
  A Garland of Sumpter Valley Days
The Gilpin Gold Tram
  Colorado's Unique Narrow Gauge
The 1871 Grant Locomotive Works
  Centennial Catalog Reproduction
Silver San Juan
  The Rio Grande Southern Railroad
West Side
  Narrow Gauge in the Sierra

Colorado & Southern Narrow Gauge
  The Beartrap Stack Era
Southern Pacific Narrow Gauge
  Loneliest and most improbable of all...
Utah & Northern
  Colorado Rail Annual No. 15
El Dorado Narrow Gauge
  The Diamond & Caldor Railway
Argent
  Last of the Swamp Rats

Second Edition
1 2 3 4 5 6 7 8 9 0

Dust Jacket: Artist Mike Pearsall has captured East Tennessee & Western North Carolina Railroad's Number 12 on an autumn afternoon at Cranberry, North Carolina in 1940.

Endsheets: A country greeting, 1938—North Carolina Department of Conservation & Development.

Train Schedule

Photo by William S. Cannon

Charles Glover "Cy" Crumley

Life is like a mountain railroad
With an engineer that's brave
We must make her run successful,
From the cradle to the grave.
We must watch for fills and tunnels,
Never falter, never quail;
Keep your hand upon the throttle,
And keep your eye upon the rail
            —American Folk Ballad

TWEETSIE COUNTRY is dedicated to Cy Crumley, who was born on July 8, 1886 at Elizabethton, Tennessee and started to work for the East Tennessee & Western North Carolina in 1906. Through the years, Cap'n Cy was responsible for not only running the narrow gauge trains, but he did so with a smile and an open heart to all those who had the fortune to ride the swaying cars, or to simply wave as she passed by. In 1913, Cy Crumley was made General Manager of the newly acquired Linville River Line and served as conductor on the first train into Boone in 1919, as well as the last in 1940. Over the years, Cy's friendly manner endeared him and the narrow gauge to all those who came in contact with the "friendliest railroad in the World".

Acknowledgments

TWEETSIE COUNTRY, as a book, started over twenty years ago, although no one, especially the author, knew it at the time. Summer ramblings into the hollows penetrated by the ET&WNC were more fun than concerted research. Interviews in those days took the form of having a "big R-C Cola" with the locals at the Shull Mills' general store and asking about the narrow gauge. However, as years passed, the research and picture-hunting became more organized, the questions more direct and the note taking more formal.

In the quest for information and illustrations about the life and times of this Blue Ridge stemwinder, the author had a great deal of help from a number of fine individuals. It is hard to delve into any short line railroad without retracing the path of the late Lucius Beebe. I am again indebted to Charles Clegg for his kindness in securing photographs made during the famous Beebe-Clegg trips of the 1940's. Robert W. Richardson came through with a wonderful assortment of photographs made both before and after the "big war."

Edward Bond was most helpful with fine historic views from his extensive collection, as were Gipson P. Vance, James P. Shuman, Steve Patterson, Lloyd D. Lewis, Henry Bender, Lawrie Brown and Hugh Morton. Other fine photographs came from Thomas Lawson, Jr., John Krause, Al and Mary Langley, W. Frank Clodfelter, John E. Parker, Jim Wade and George H. Gregory.

The artwork in TWEETSIE COUNTRY is by Mike Pearsall and M. W. Holtzinger, two young leaders in the field of railroad painting. Scale drawings are from the drafting tables of John E. Robinson and David Braun, both dedicated draftsmen as well as modelmakers.

Many questions were answered by former engineman Sherman Pippin. Cy Crumley was always willing to dig up one more obscure detail or photograph. ET&WNC vice-president K. E. Wilhoit, former vice-president J. E. Vance and president Alfred Steel provided invaluable materials from the company's files, while former employees Dayton Simerly, Mack Luctral, C. C. "Brownie" Allison, George F. Allison and R. S. Bowling brought up facts most people had forgotten. C. Grattan Price, Jr. and the late Grover C. Robbins, Jr. told of their efforts to both save and operate a part of Tweetsie for future generations.

The late H. Temple Crittenden, Jack Alexander, Reverend Bill Gwaltney, and Hugh G. Boutell were most helpful with photographs. Francis H. Parker has explored the area in depth and provided additional information. Other historical data came from the Southern Historical Collection of the University of North

Carolina and from Charlotte T. Ross, the curator of the Appalachian Collection at Appalachian State University. Published materials are listed in the bibliography.

Proofreading was accomplished by Reverend Jud van Gorder, Gordon Chappell, Robert W. Richardson and William S. Cannon. It was Bill Cannon who prodded the author when his motivation was low and once he had my attention, continued to ask such leading questions that I had no choice but to dig deeper for the answers. Bill Cannon was a driving force and inspiritation throughout the years.

Some of the finest photographs are from the camera of former TRAINS staffer and good friend Robert B. Adams. More help came from William M. Moedinger, Vince Ryan, Ted Schnepf, Capt. Henry C. Bridges, Jr. and Archie L. Julian. Uncredited photographs are from the author's collection, or camera.

One word of thanks to my new wife Gloria, who has endured bouncing back-road trips, remote and picturesque picnics and somewhat less than first class accomodations . . . may you never learn the difference between a cowcatcher and a caboose and may you be happy not knowing.

The East Tennessee & Western North Carolina Railroad's Number 12 sends the echo of her exhaust across the valley as she doubles State Line Hill near Elk Park, North Carolina in January 1946. The classic photograph was made by Charles M. Clegg.

Introduction

Tweetsie Country can be roughly defined as being bounded on the North by the Great Depression, and the east by the state of North Carolina, on the west by Tennessee and on the south by hope and determination. It has been a long time since I left those hills, but I must admit that they are still a part of me and will be always.

For the purist, Tweetsie Country is that remote part of Western North Carolina and Northeastern Tennessee, just below the Virginia state line at the crest of that part of the Appalachian Mountains known as the Blue Ridge. It is an area given over largely to rhododendron covered mountains, black bear and a few small towns. The crafts of soap making, weaving, moonshining, and five-string banjo picking are still practiced there in their orginal forms.

The people of this area, isolated from the busy world and somewhat lost in time, led a simple life until relatively recent times. Sure, they remembered the wars . . . their men folk had gone off to fight in each of them, the Civil, Spanish-American and the two world wars. They recalled all too well the Great Depression,

for it was there long before it had a fancy $5 bureaucratic name, and it lingers in some hollows until this very day. An elderly gentleman in Roan Mountain, Tennessee said: "T'ain't the depression by itself that's so bad, hit's coming right on top of the Civil War seems to make it mor'n we can stand." This typified the sentiments of the hill people well into this century.

The people of the Blue Ridge Mountains also remember a small narrow gauge train that twisted and turned its way through the hills from Johnson City, over Tennessee way, to Boone, North Carolina. Through the years the East Tennessee & Western North Carolina Railroad, although few knew it by its formal name, and its offspring, the Linville River Railway, threaded its way into the hearts of all those who saw its daily passing for over seventy years. At one time the railroad did a good business in lumber and iron ore. But soon the hillsides were scarred and bare and the depression years saw all too many proud families on welfare.

In the 1880's, the railroad was called "Stemwinder." Later the road was known as the "Eat Taters & Wear No Clothes," but it was the children who rode the swaying cars to numerous summer camps around Linville and Grandfather Mountain who gave the railroad a name that lasted . . . Tweetsie. The summer children could hear the Shrill whistles of the tiny Baldwin ten wheelers as they chuffed up the gorge . . . making a "tweet" sound.

Everyone held the Tweetsie in high esteem, but like the people she served, Tweetsie never had much money. In later years she made do with mixed trains of cord wood, coal and a combination car divided into four parts for baggage, United States Mail and passengers, both white and colored. The affection that the East Tennessee & Western North Carolina held is hard to define. Perhaps old Mrs. Judkins at Linville Gap hit upon the real reason when she said: "It's the onliest train there is around here."

So here comes Tweetsie, its broad gauge aspirations on a narrow gauge budget, its tobacco "chawing" passengers, sunny picnic trains, sudden disastrous rains, good days and hard times . . . stand back folks and watch her pass.

— Mallory Hope Ferrell

Train Time at Elk Park, 1941 — Robert B. Adams

Foreword

Stemwinder

The passenger train that curls its volume of smoke through and beyond the beautiful vales of the Watauga is called by the quaint but appropriate nomenclature of the stemwinder, because in winding the many graceful curves of the road where brooks pouring down over the rocks throw spray in at the windows, and the passing gales blossom with sweet odors of the woods, it bears a marked resemblance to the tempered steel of the timekeeper in playing its part within the glittering gold and among the intricate movements of the best jewelled stemwinder in the pocket of the millionaire.

From *The Balsam Groves of the Grandfather Mountain*
    By Shepherd Monroe Dugger, 1892.

Robert B. Adams

1

Broad Gauge Days

The events that led to the eventual construction of the East Tennessee & Western North Carolina Railroad date back to the period following the War of 1812, a time when the Blue Ridge Mountain country of western North Carolina and Eastern Tennessee was the American frontier. This was Daniel Boone's country; it was remote and sparsely inhabited. The mountain vastness was still the hunting ground of the Cherokee Nation. Civilization had followed the major rivers; bypassing these mountains.

The discovery of iron ore in these hills had an odd beginning. Three brothers, Joshua, Ben and Jake Perkins of Crab Orchard, Tennessee had attended a "log rolling" near that township and a scuffle followed the feast. The men attempted to remove the new flax shirt of one, Wright Moreland and in the process injured his pride. Moreland was angered sufficiently to obtain warrants for the arrest of the Perkins boys. To escape prosecution, the men fled to the nearby mountains of North Carolina, where they supported themselves by digging for and selling a rare herb known as "ginseng."[1] In their search for the root, they discovered a vein of magnetite iron ore, near what was later called Cranberry, North Carolina.[2]

The Perkins brothers' find was reputed to be the richest vein of magnetite known in America at that time. It was the first discovery in what would become known as the "Cranberry Iron Belt." This belt stretches for about twenty-two miles from near Cranberry, in a southwesterly direction to the Toe River, crossing the undulating state line several times in the process.

Very little written history of this region has been recorded. Many stories have been passed down to later generations, in the form of tales and ballads. Even today the mountain fastness is the last stronghold of pure Americana, mainly in the form of crafts, folk music and legend.

The *Iron Manufacturer's Guide* for 1859 tells about three iron furnaces in the area. The Cranberry Bloomery Forge[3] was constructed on Cranberry Creek in 1820. It was rebuilt and enlarged in 1856 and boasted two fires and one

[1]*A flowering plant used in folk medicine.*

[2]*Magnetite is a very rich type of iron ore, accompanied by a variety of pyroxene salite malcalite, making it most suited for making steel by the acid process.*

The Original 5-foot gauge ET&WNC planned to connect with the equally broad gauge Western North Carolina RR to form a Trans-Appalachian route. — N.C. State Archives

1

hammer. The following year the forge produced 17 tons of wrought iron bars. Five miles south of the Cranberry Forge was the Toe River Bloomery Forge, built in 1843. This bloomery also had two fires and a hammer and made about four tons of iron bars in 1856. Johnson's Bloomery Forge, located some six miles south of Cranberry was started in 1841 and made a ton and a half of blooms in 1856. These three "Bloomeries" utilized ore mined on the site from outcroppings in the "Cranberry Iron Belt."

By 1859 the Cranberry Bloomery Forge was known as the Cranberry Iron Company, owned by Twitty, Miller and Bynum and leased to Jordan C. Hardin. This firm owned approximately 4,000 acres of land, including a smelter and the facilities used in making blooms and pig iron.

Peter Hardin was hauling iron ore from the Cranberry Forge to Camp Vance, some distance south of Morganton, North Carolina, during the Civil War. This iron was destined for the Confederate forces. It is interesting to note that Peter Hardin was one of John Hardin's Negro slaves. During the war between the states, iron ore was also hauled to Johnson's Depot, Tennessee, Lenoir and Marion, North Carolina. Sympathy in the hills was anti-slavery and a Confederate garrison was ambushed near Banner Elk during the war.

A post office was established at Cranberry Forge in 1861 with John Hardin as Post Master. Later, on January 11, 1881, Peter Hardin was appointed to the post by Horance Maynard, then Postmaster General.

After the war, in 1866, E. Nye Hutchinson purchased the Cranberry Iron Company and on February 28, 1873, General R. F. Hoke bought the works and formed the Cranberry Iron & Coal Company. Sherman Pippin, long time resident, former East Tennessee & Western North Carolina Railroad engineer and local sage, recalls that Hoke purchased the entire township "for a little gray mare and a rifle gun." The story is probably more legend than fact, but interesting nonetheless.

General Hoke's partners included William Murdock, Moses L. Holmes, M. C. Beatty and C. W. Russell. Capital stock in the amount of $200,000 was subscribed to by Hoke, Ario Pardee, William Firmstone, J. G. Fell, Calvin Pardee, Ario Pardee, Jr., George Richards and Franklin A. Comly. The new firm took over operation of the forge on February 25, 1874. Pardee and his associates controlled vast quantities of coal and iron and were headquartered at Philadelphia, Pennsylvania.

It is interesting to note that at this very same time Ario Pardee was busy building the narrow gauge East Broad Top Railroad out of Mount Union, Pennsylvania. He had similar plans for his new southern interest. The East Broad Top would be the only narrow gauge common carrier east of the Rockies to outlive the East Tennessee & Western North Carolina and they would each have a common board member for as long as they ran.

In order to get the iron ore from the mountains, a transportation system would be needed. The East Tennessee & Western North Carolina Railroad Company was chartered by the Tennessee General Assembly on May 24, 1866. The capital stock was set at $30,000 in shares of $25 each. Incorporators of the line were all local men. The broad gauge railroad was intended to run from "either Carter or Johnson's Depot" on the East Tennessee & Virginia Railroad, to Elizabethton, Doe River Cove, Crab Orchard and to the Cranberry Iron Works, just over the state line in North Carolina.

[3] A "bloom" is a mass of wrought iron from a forge or puddling furnance. Iron works were often known as a bloomery.

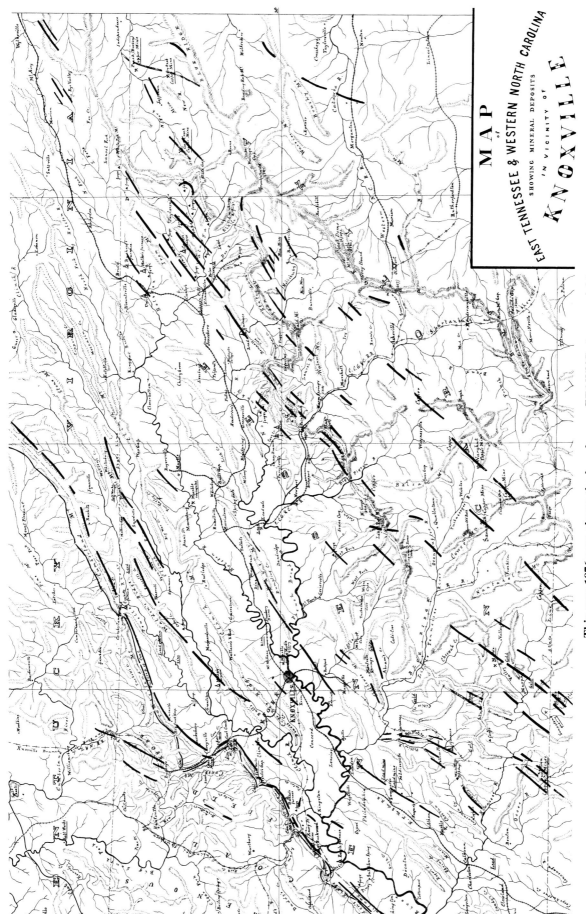

This rare 1876 map shows the broad gauge ET&WNC at upper right.

The charter allowed the new railroad company two years in which to commence the work. Stock was sold at Elizabethton, Carter Depot, Johnson's Depot, Doe River Cove and Taylorsville (now Mountain City), Tennessee. The legislature authorized Carter County to take stock in the railroad in an amount "not exceeding $50,000." Johnson County was also allowed to purchase stock in the project.

The East Tennessee & Western North Carolina Railroad was authorized to draw bonds from the State of Tennessee in the amount of $10,000 per mile in order to "iron and equipt said road." Under this provision, President E. Simerly was authorized, on March 26, 1868, to obtain $150,000 in state bonds for the purpose of grading. Two months after an additional $100,000 was obtained for the bridge building, while on January 1, 1869, Simerly obtained another $150,000 in state bonds. A total of $400,000 in bonds was thus obtained and sold for $260,132.17. These were common financial dealings for new railroads during this period. A railroad would obtain state bonds and sell them for what they could, using the cash to build the railroad.

Records of the original East Tennessee & Western North Carolina are both sketchy and rare. The original minute books state that Chief Engineer C.A. Mee completed his survey in the spring of 1867. Johnson's Depot was considered to be the better terminal for the five-foot gauge road. Construction was commenced in the spring of 1868 and the grade was partially completed between Johnson City (the "Depot" had been dropped) and Hampton, Tennessee in the summer of 1869. Some tracklaying and bridge work was underway on February 28, 1870, but work went slowly and money was always in short supply. At this time, the board of directors consisted of Lawson W. Hampton, John Hughes, J.M. Johnson, E. Simerly, I.A. Taylor, J.C. Hardin and E.W. Heaton.

On November 15, 1871, the State of Tennessee declared the East Tennessee & Western North Carolina Railroad Company to be delinquent and its railroad, rights and franchises were sold by the commissioners[4] to John Hughes and others for $20,000 in bonds of the State. Hughes had been one of the original founders of the road in 1866 and headed a group made up of E. Simerly, S.W. Williams, A.E. Jackson, C.P. Tonckrey, J.K. Miller, H.C. Smith, W.B. Haynes, N.M. Taylor, J.C. Hardin, R.R. Butler and Lawson Clifford.

On November 13, 1874, the commissioners reported that the money had been paid and on November 18th, the title was transferred to John Hughes and his partners. Hughes became president and J.C. Hardin was named secretary-treasurer.

At this time it was planned to extend the East Tennessee & Western North Carolina Railroad to the western extension of the North Carolina Railroad. However, no further work was accomplished on the incomplete grade and the road was still without locomotives or rolling stock. The ET&WNC had only been able to lay five miles of 52 pound iron "T" rail on the grade out of Johnson City. It never owned any rolling stock and trackage got no further than Watauga Point, west of Elizabethton.

The only recorded operations over the five foot gauge East Tennessee & Western North Carolina commenced in November 1872, when the East Tennessee, Virginia & Georgia Railroad (now Southern Railway) ran several trains over the ET&WNC "to remove the rock on each side of said railroad that is in John H. Bowman's field near William Wheeler's." An agreement gave the large road the

[4]Commission composed of Tennessee Governor John C. Brown, Secretary of State Charles N. Gibbs, Comptroller John C. Birch and Francis B. Fogg.

right to cut the ET&WNC track and lay a side track to the rock and also to "use the scattering of cross ties at Johnson City, belonging to said company, excepting for the ties for the switch, on the condition that it has them neatly cross-piled again without seriously damaging the same." The Wheeler farm was located near the site of the east switch to the Johnson City yards, less than a mile from a connection with the larger road.

"Narrow Gauge Fever" was in epidemic proportions across the Nation. Out in Colorado, General William Jackson Palmer was pushing his fledgling Denver & Rio Grande from Denver toward Mexico City, proving that a three-foot gauge railroad was both practical and economical.

On April 21, 1874 J.C. Hardin wrote his friend Colonel J. Roswell King of Rossville, Georgia:

> **We have some four hundred tons of T-rail weighing fifty two pounds per lineal yard, which we wish to sell, as we wish to change the gauge of our road to a narrow gauge so we have the above amount of new iron railing we wish to dispose of.**

On September 10, 1875, Ario Pardee and his associates purchased the abandoned East Tennessee & Western North Carolina Railroad for $25,000.[5] Pardee had purchased the Cranberry Iron Works in 1873 and formed the Cranberry Iron & Coal Company. Now he had the means to get his iron ore to the outside world.

Thus, Ario Pardee, Jr. became president of the East Tennessee & Western North Carolina with a board consisting of his father, Ario, Franklin Comly, William Firmstone, George Richards, Robert Franklin Hoke and J.C. Hardin. The railroad and the iron company were now in the same hands and the conversion to narrow gauge was an important part of the plan.

This rare view shows the only train to operate over the broad gauge ET&WNC in November 1872.—Sherman Pippin

[5]*The purchase was not approved and monies paid until February 16, 1876.*

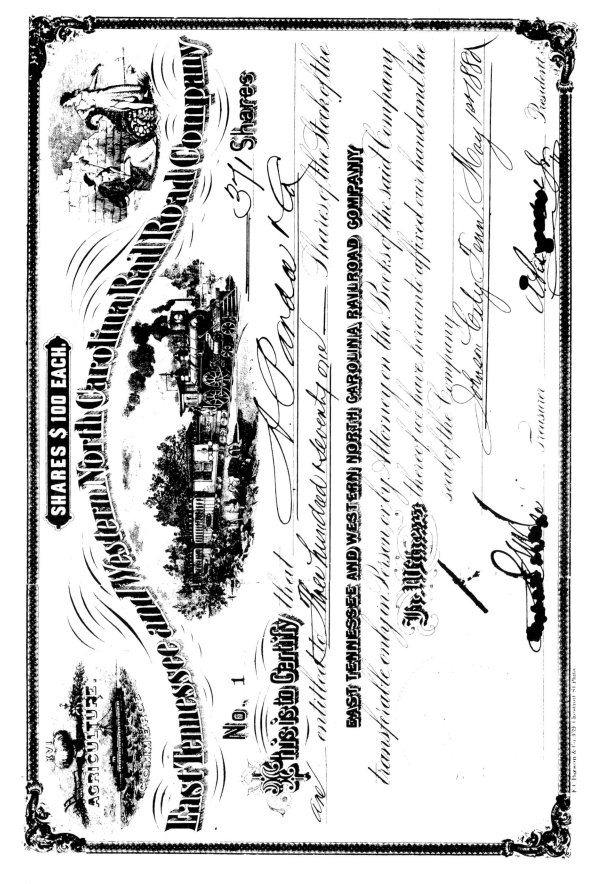

East Tennessee and Western North Carolina Rail Road Company

SHARES $100 EACH.

AGRICULTURE.
COMMERCE.

371 Shares

No. 1

This is to Certify that

entitled to Three Hundred seventy one — Shares of the Stock of the

EAST TENNESSEE AND WESTERN NORTH CAROLINA RAILROAD COMPANY

transferable only in Person or by Attorney on the Books of the said Company

thereof as have hereunto affixed our hand and the

seal of the Company

Johnson City, Tenn, May 1st 1882

Treasurer

President

F. C. Pozzoni & Co. 430 Chestnut St Phila

6

2

Narrow Gauge to Cranberry

When Ario Pardee and General Robert Franklin Hoke and their associates took over the East Tennessee & Western North Carolina Railroad in 1875, the road consisted of five miles of iron "T" rail extending from Johnson City to Watauga Point, west of Elizabethton, Tennessee. Grading for the five-foot gauge line was partially complete as far east as Doe River Cove, but the railroad had no equipment and had never begun operation, despite the work of the past ten years. A stockholders' meeting was held in Johnson City on May 22, 1879, at which time the title of the ET&WNC broad gauge was handed over to Pardee by John Hughes.

The decision had already been made to rebuild the East Tennessee & Western North Carolina as a three foot, narrow gauge road. Pardee had seen the advantages of narrow gauge construction and operation on his East Broad Top Railroad & Coal Company in Pennsylvania. A 2-6-0 mogul-type locomotive was ordered from the Baldwin Locomotive Works in Philadelphia and orders for both freight and passenger equipment were placed with the car builders.

In the meantime, the railroad retained the services of Colonel Thomas E. Matson to act as Chief Engineer and Superintendent of the line. Ario Pardee, in a letter to J.C. Hardin dated October 29, 1879, stated:

> **General Hoke will come across the mountains from Morganton (N.C.) about the time Mr. Matson will reach the road. If he should be detained we will be obligated to you if you will give Mr. Matson all the information you can in reference to the topography of the county.**

Colonel Matson began his location work to Cranberry in early November, 1879. The company desired the shortest line that could be built, but questioned if it was possible to run a line through the Doe River Gorge. The only alternative would be to build a longer route up the Little Doe River, over Whitehead's Hill and down again into the valley of the Doe. Matson worked throughout the winter and early spring and was able to locate a route through the gorge by utilizing four percent grades and 32 degree curves with four tunnels and three large bridges over the Doe. The cliffs of the Doe River were so steep that at one location in the gorge, Colonel Matson had to lower men, equipment and mules into the gorge with block and tackle in order to work on the tunnels from both portals. Tunnel work was

Stock certificate Number 1, to Ario Pardee & Company, was the first to be issued by the narrow gauge ET&WNC.

accomplished with black powder, manual labor and small mules.

The grading and masonry contract was awarded to Joseph H. Lofrode and Francis H. Saylor on August 26, 1880. Later in the year the same men were given a contract to build the truss bridges. New 40 pound rail began arriving at Johnson City in January, 1881 and an East Tennessee, Virginia & Georgia train brought in a narrow gauge mogul with the name "Watauga" neatly lettered above the cab panels. Watauga is the Cherokee Indian word for beautiful, and the trim Number 1 was just that! Ed Tally had been hired as the first engineer and soon the "Watauga" was engaged in carrying rails, ties and track materials to the easterly advancing railhead.

Near Hampton, Tennessee, hard rock crews were completing a 289-foot tunnel that had been started in broad gauge days, but never completed. Just outside the tunnel, the bridge crews of Lofrode & Saylor were completing an equally long Howe Truss covered bridge of native timber. The three span bridge over the Doe River would stand as an East Tennessee landmark for as long as the narrow gauge ran.

The 14.1 miles of line from Johnson City to Hampton were completed in the late summer and the line was opened for service on August 22, 1881. The first train was hauled by the "Watauga" and consisted of combine Number 1 and coach Number 2, with several flats filled with the overflow crowd. Another Baldwin 2-6-0 had just arrived and it was named the "Cranberry." Brown Davis was hired to run her.

During the eight months following completion of the East Tennessee & Western North Carolina as far as Hampton, the road carried 7,701 passengers and received $2,671.90, an average of 34½ cents per passenger, traveling an average distance of 8½ miles. The road also carried 3,074 tons of freight and received $1.28 per ton on an average haul of 6 miles. Equipment consisted of the two locomotives ("Watauga" and "Cranberry"), one combination car, one passenger coach, five box cars, six gondolas, 23 flats, four hand cars and two push cars "all in good condition and running order."

East of Hampton lay 19.3 miles of rugged country, before the mine at Cranberry could be reached. Just east of town, a conventional Howe Truss covered bridge was used to cross the Little Doe River and gain entry into the deep Doe River Gorge. The road climbed 1,500 feet between Johnson City and Hampton, most of the climb being east of Elizabethton. However, the real climb lay ahead.

The Doe River Gorge is one of the deepest and most primitive gorges in the eastern United States. From river rock to the top of the granite cliff is a sheer climb of almost one thousand feet and the narrow profile leaves little room for a railroad. The base of the gorge is covered in season by crimson rhododendron, flaming azalea and many mountain wild flowers.

It was through this narrow defile, with the river on one side and the near vertical rock cliffs on the other, that Colonel Matson chose to locate the East Tennessee & Western North Carolina's tracks. The roadbed snaked along a narrow shelf, blasted from the rock walls during 1881 and 1882. The grade was a steady four percent and when the white water Doe twisted even too much for the slim gauge rails, Matson used bridges and tunnels. East of Pardee Point, the track crossed a bridge, entered a tunnel and crossed another truss bridge on a steady climb.

Of the five rock tunnels on the East Tennessee & Western North Carolina, four were located in the Doe River Gorge, the fifth was at the east end of the deck-type covered bridge near Hampton. Despite the problems associated with a scarcity of labor, inclement weather and rugged terrain, the minutes of the Board

9

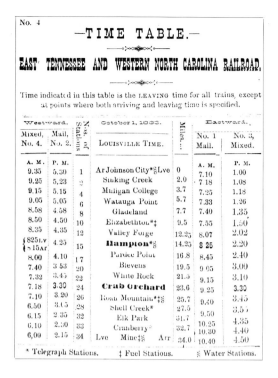

—TIME TABLE.—

EAST TENNESSEE AND WESTERN NORTH CAROLINA RAILROAD.

Time indicated in this table is the LEAVING time for all trains, except at points where both arriving and leaving time is specified.

Westward.		Nos. of Stations	October 1, 1883.	Miles	Eastward.	
Mixed, No. 4.	Mail, No. 2.		LOUISVILLE TIME.		No. 1 Mail.	No. 3, Mixed.
A. M.	P. M.				A. M.	P. M.
9.35	5.30	1	Ar Johnson City*§Lve	0	7.10	1.00
9.25	5.23	2	Sinking Creek	2.0	7.18	1.08
9.15	5.15	4	Milligan College	3.7	7.25	1.18
9.05	5.05	6	Watauga Point	5.7	7.33	1.26
8.58	4.58	8	Gladeland	7.7	7.40	1.35
8.50	4.50	10	Elizabethton*‡	9.5	7.55	1.50
8.35	4.35	12	Valley Forge	12.25	8.07	2.02
8.25Lv / 8.15Ar	4.25	15	**Hampton***§	14.25	8.25	2.20
8.00	4.10	17	Pardee Point	16.8	8.45	2.40
7.40	3.53	20	Blevens	19.5	9.05	3.00
7.32	3.45	22	White Rock	21.5	9.15	3.10
7.18	3.30	24	**Crab Orchard**	23.6	9.25	3.30
7.10	3.20	26	Roan Mountain*‡§	25.7	9.40	3.45
6.50	3.05	28	Shell Creek*	27.5	9.50	3.55
6.15	2.35	32	Elk Park	31.7	10.25	4.35
6.10	2.30	33	Cranberry	32.7	10.30	4.40
6.00	2.15	34	Lve Mine‡§ Arr	34.0	10.40	4.50

* Telegraph Stations.   ‡ Fuel Stations.   § Water Stations.

Conductors and Engineers are prohibited from runing trains without having this time table in their possession.

Trains will wait on each other at all meeting or passing points thirty (30) minutes.

Trains will leave terminal stations regardless of over-due trains Such over-due trains must keep entirely out of the way.

No delayed train shall attempt to run to a meeting point after it gets twenty-five (25) minutes behind its regular time.

Construction trains must be on siding, and have tracks clear, at least ten (10) minutes ahead of regular trains.

Switches must be reset for main track immediately after train passes in or out of siding.

Conductors and Engineers will compare time daily with clock in the office at Johnson City.

When, from any cause, a train is delayed the schedule time is as fast as it should run, but such train must not, under any circumstances, run at a higher rate of speed than fifteen (15) miles per hour.

Through the "Gorge," and at all points where rock or land slides are possible, and in descending heavy grades, trains must be kept under perfect control, and speed must not exceed six (6) miles per hour.

All stations, or other points where trains are liable to be standing, must be approached with train under full control.

No. 1 and No. 2 shall have the right of track, and all other trains will side track for them when practicable.

"Enterprise" Job Rooms, Johnson City, Tenn.

The oldest existing timetable went into effect October 15, 1883 and gave special rules. The view below shows trackage in the Doe River Gorge in August of 1881. William S. Cannon. **Engine No. 1 is shown in the Gorge (opposite page) in 1883.** — Ed Bond Collection.

of Directors' meeting held on May 17, 1882, show that Matson's crews had completed most of the grading, except a "small amount of material in a cut near the terminus" at Cranberry. Colonel Matson said that the bridges were complete except for two spans and that a great deal of work had been done on the older portions of the road, including widening cuts and removing material "liable to produce a landslide." Rails reached Elk Park over in North Carolina, and the first train brought in Doctor Abram Jobe and his family on June 13, 1882. Cranberry was now only a little over one mile away.

The directors made plans to open the entire line from Johnson City to Cranberry on July 1, 1882. The new line would require more motive power and the directors placed an order with the Baldwin Works for a new, larger locomotive, a 2-8-0 consolidation type to be numbered 3 and named the "Unaka."

The line to Cranberry was officially opened on July 3, 1882. Daily freight and passenger service was begun the following day. Depots had been built at Hampton, Roan Mountain and Cranberry. The narrow gauge used the ETV&G depot at Johnson City. Sidings were put in at Elizabethton and Hampton, while Johnson City and Cranberry both boasted a small yard. Water tanks were built at Johnson City, Hampton, Roan Mountain and at the mine.

With the arrival of the narrow gauge, systematic and large scale mining was undertaken at the Cranberry mine, located just four miles over the North Carolina state line. In the spring of 1884 the company "blew-in" a small blast furnace. The furnace was 50 feet high and had a capacity of 14 to 15 tons of iron per day. Between 1884 and 1893 about 200,000 tons of ore were mined, averaging 40 to 50 percent metallic iron.

By 1892, the workings of the Cranberry Iron & Coal Company covered over seven acres and the daily output of the mine was about 40 tons of iron ore. Two main tunnels tapped the main ore body, while mining continued on four other open cuts.

Masses of ore and rock were first broken down by air-drilling and blasting. Rock and lean ore were then loaded on tram cars, drawn by mules and dumped on waste piles. High grade ore was then conveyed in a wooden chute to the ore platforms at the foot of the hill beside the railroad tracks. Ore being shipped out over the narrow gauge was first hand picked and then loaded in the ET&WNC cars by shovel. The ore was shipped to Johnson City where the Virginia Iron, Coal & Coke Company operated a large blast furnace at the end of a three rail joint spur track used by the ET&WNC and the by then standard gauge ETV&G. Freight to Johnson City cost 70 cents per ton. Ore going to the Cranberry furnace was treated by magnetic concentration, after crushing to golf-ball size. The ore was then washed, sorted and sent to the furnace. Prior to 1890 the furnace burned charcoal, but coke was found to provide better heat. Limestone came from Watauga Point, where the Cranberry Iron & Coal Company operated a quarry. Finished iron was shipped to furnaces and steel mills in Ohio and Pennsylvania, most of it being used in the manufacture of high quality crucible tool steel.

With the issuance of the timetable Number 4, effective October 15, 1883, operations on the East Tennessee & Western North Carolina had assumed a regular pattern with the three locomotives handling all of the traffic on the 34 mile road. Each morning saw "The Mail" scheduled to leave Johnson City at 7:10, arriving at Cranberry three and a half hours later. "Mixed Number 3" left at 1:00 p.m. and arrived at Cranberry at 4:50 p.m. "The Mail" whistled off for Johnson City at 2:15 following a lunch break at the mine and arrived home at 5:30 in the evening. "Mixed train 4" departed Cranberry at 6:00 p.m. and arrived in Johnson City at

Baldwin 2-6-0 Number 2, the "Cranberry" powers a construction train in 1882. — William S. Cannon from Cy Crumley Coll. **The Cranberry Mine itself is shown (below). Note the W. M. Ritter Lumber Co. Shay at left.** — L. A. Tolley Coll.

East Tennessee & Western North Carolina
RAILROAD COMPANY.

Detail of Voucher No. 209.

To *Wallace Hahn*

December 1883

$ 100 00/100

Charge, *General Expenses*.

ACCOUNT OF

1 *Salaries* .100 00

2

3

4

5

Total, 100 00

Correct: *Wallace Hahn* Auditor.

Ario Pardee was the driving force behind the ET&WNC as well as the East Broad Top Railroad in Pennsylvania. — Lee Rainey Coll.

9:35 each evening. As a rule, the moguls held down passenger and mixed runs while the heavier 2-8-0 was generally assigned to freight trains. The East Tennessee & Western North Carolina purchased no more new engines during the nineteenth century. However the original crosshead pumps were replaced by injectors and the original wood fuel was replaced by coal in the late 1890's, the engines being equipped with straight stacks and extended smokeboxes at about this same time.

East Tennessee & Western North Carolina trains were dispatched by telegraph over a single strand of wire put up in the summer of 1882. The railroad company provided chestnut poles and labor, while the Western Union Telegraph Company provided the wire and insulators. The Stemwinder and the telegraph firm shared the line, with the narrow gauge having priority for its use.

The beginning of train service opened up the vast and beautiful country to the outside world. In 1885, General John T. Wilder built a huge 166-room hotel atop Roan Mountain and called the resort "Cloudland." Wilder had seen the beautiful slopes of the Roan during his Civil War service and had returned to erect the impressive three story structure. The "Cloudland" was 200 feet long and 80 feet wide. The state line ran across the maple flooring of the ballroom and both the great and the near-do-wells came to partake of its elegence.

Sherman Pippin once drove a hack from the East Tennessee & Western North Carolina depot to the "Cloudland." Since he washed his blankets once a week in the creek, he received all of the business from women passengers. On one trip his passengers included several ladies and it was a very hot summer day. Also on board was a cask of whiskey destined for the hotel's oak bar. Everyone was especially thirsty, so Sherman took a penknife and bored a small hole in the bottom of the barrel, making a plug to fit the hole. Everyone quenched his thirst and as Sherman neared the top of the mountain, he drove the plug into the hole, covered

14

Purple Rhododendron cover the slopes of 6,313 foot Roan Mountain, once the site of the huge Cloudland Hotel.

it with a little dirt and no one ever knew the difference.

In order to pay a debt to the parent Cranberry Iron & Coal Company, the East Tennessee & Western North Carolina Railroad was forced to sell the four miles of trackage located in North Carolina to the iron company on January 1, 1894. The ET&WNC purchased this trackage back again on August 15, 1905. Operations were not affected by the financial maneuver.

Railroads were the subject of many late evening conversations in the Blue Ridge hills and a number of "paper railroads" were reported in the trade press. *Railway Age* told of one in May 1890: The Cranberry & Linville Railroad was projected from the ET&WNC's end of track to Linville, North Carolina, 13 miles, by J. R. Erwin and Hugh MacRae. The MacRae family owned huge stands of timber in the Grandfather Mountain area and, while the Cranberry & Linville Railroad failed to get past the planning stage, Hugh MacRae later built his own narrow gauge logging line out of Linville and powered his line with diminutive Shay and Climax locomotives.

The dual gauge trackage of the Johnson City yards are shown in these two glimpses from 1903. Artist Mike Pearsall captures the crew of Number 3, while the Baldwin 2-8-0 is shown in a glass plate view from J. T. Dowdy. — Ed Bond Collection.

17

Mike Pearsall

ET&WNC No. 3 poses with her crew at Shell Creek in 1882.—Bill Cannon from Cy Crumley Collection.

Later in 1890, the *Railway Gazette* reported another railroad connection for the East Tennessee & Western North Carolina. In its issue of October 10th of that year, the *Gazette* stated that the Watauga Valley Railroad would be built from "Watauga Point to South Johnson City." On November 7, 1890, the same sheet reported that the line would extend five miles from Carter's Station (once Watauga) to Watauga Point and that the contract had been awarded to Durand & Murphy. The report was followed by the remark so typical with paper railroads: "work to commence at once." About one mile of grading was actually accomplished on this road, which was owned by the East Tennessee Mining & Improvement Company. It is possible that a portion of this grade was used by the ET&WNC in 1910, when they constructed their "Buffalo Bridge Branch," later known as the Watauga River Spur. This branch was constructed with three rails for both narrow and standard gauge operations.

In 1898, the first of many private feeder railroads was constructed. That year the Forge Mining Company built a three mile, three-foot gauge railroad from near Roan Mountain, up Doe River to Forge Branch. The mining firm purchased a small Baldwin 0-6-0T engine from an iron mine at Embreeville, Tennessee. The former Embreeville Furnace Company engine was put in service between the ET&WNC connection and the mine. The engine was numbered 1, but she was always called "Add," after a Roan Mountain lady of the night. One old timer remarked that the little saddle tanker ran like a "high stepping whore." The Forge Mining Company encountered financial difficulties and in 1899 the property was leased to the Cranberry Iron & Coal Company. The branch was used very little after that time and the engine was used briefly at the Cranberry Mine before being sold to the Flint Knob Mine near Maymead, Tennessee. The old Forge Mining railroad was torn up following the May flood of 1901, which destroyed all of the ET&WNC bridges in the Doe River Gorge and halted through train service for several months.

In 1896, the three Camp brothers of Chicago came to western North Carolina in order to develop a large stand of white pine timber located east of Cranberry, near the crest of the Blue Ridge Mountains. The Camps projected a 12-mile narrow gauge railroad from Cranberry and the East Tennessee & Western North Carolina to their sawmill at Saginaw, North Carolina. The Camps built a hotel at Saginaw and incorporated their railroad on July 13, 1896. The name of the town was changed to Pineola and after some grading, the project was in debt, subsequently failed and went into receivership.

Mogul No. 2 derailed in the Johnson City yards in 1904. Engineer Scot Dean and fireman Bellmot Watson were not injured in the turn-over.—Ed Bond Collection.

Times were getting rough in the hill country. Revenues were down for the East Tennessee & Western North Carolina and the road was forced to do away with regular passenger trains and exist with mixed trains and meager earnings for awhile. However, brighter days lay ahead for the Stemwinder.

CRANBERRY, N.C.

1892

El. 3219 (at station point)   M.P. 33.4 (from Johnson City, Tennessee)

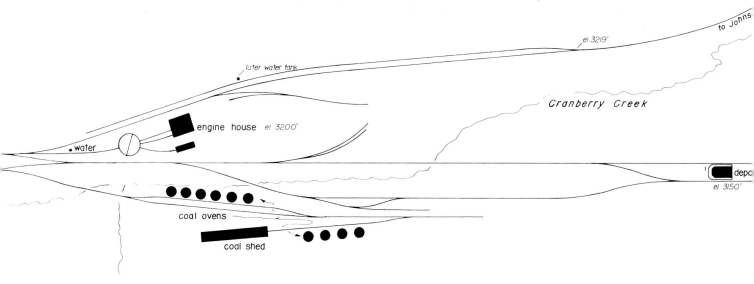

to Johns

el 3219'

Cranberry Creek

later water tank

engine house   el 3200'

water

depo

el 3150'

coal ovens

coal shed

note: mining facilities not shown.

drawn by DAVID W. BRAUN   1974   scale 1" = 100'

Cranberry, North Carolina was the focal point for operations over the ET&WNC and later the Linville River. For it was here that the largest iron mine was located. ET&WNC Number 1 is shown at Cranberry in about 1907. The mainline hugs the hillside in the background. — George Allison Coll. The map shows the switchback and trackage in 1892. — Drawing by David W. Braun. The Cranberry depot is shown (above) in 1941, while 4-wheel caboose 205 poses in 1910 at Cranberry. — Ed Bond Coll.

EAST TENNESSEE AND WESTERN NORTH CAROLINA RAILROAD AND LINVILLE RIVER RAILWAY

The Scenic Route through *The Heart of the Blue Ridge*

24

—Hugh Morton Collection.

Linville River Line

With the arrival of the East Tennessee & Western North Carolina Railroad, the timber on the Blue Ridge mountainsides was more readily available to the hungry saws of the lumbermen. As early as 1890 there was talk of narrow gauge railroads that would connect with the East Tennessee & Western North Carolina and tap the timber resources. That year, Hugh MacRae and J.R. Erwin projected the Cranberry & Linville Railroad, but the line never got beyond the planning stage. Years later MacRae would build a privately owned narrow gauge logging line out of Linville, North Carolina and power it with several Shay and Climax geared locomotives.

Some small scale lumbering had been going on in the area for many years, the small circle mills producing mine timbers and lumber for the local citizens as well as acid wood and tan bark. One of these sawmills was operated by Dolliver & Nagel in an area that had come to be called Saginaw. Early in 1896, the three Camp brothers of Chicago came South and acquired ownership of a large stand of white pine east of Cranberry. The Linville River Railroad was incorporated by Everette H. Camp on July 13, 1896 to construct a railroad from Cranberry to the mill site at Saginaw, North Carolina. The projected railroad would "run about 12 miles."

Construction was begun on the railroad during the summer of 1896 and a small hotel was built at Saginaw. This hotel was near the sawmill and was operated by Mrs. Lewellen Penland. Mrs. Penland had a small daughter named Ola and when it came time to select a name for the hotel. Everette Camp combined the words "pine" and "Ola" to form Pineola. The Post Office Department, at the request of Camp, officially changed the name of the sawmill town from Saginaw to Pineola.

During construction of the Linville River Railroad grade in 1896, a local bootlegger furnished many of the laborers with illicit whiskey, bartering his brew for Arbuckle coffee. This particular brand of coffee, produced by the Arbuckle Brothers of New York, offered a variety of merchandise in exchange for the paper wrappers from their cans. Within a short time, natives dubbed the new railroad as the "Arbuckle Coffee Line." It was a name which stuck for several decades and is still spoken of by hillbilly bards in the deepest hollows.

After initial grading had begun out of Cranberry, construction activity on the Linville River Railroad ceased. Talk was that the Camps had either run out of money or lost interest in the project.

The timber was still untouched and in the summer of 1898, noted lumber baron William M. Ritter of Welch, West Virginia, sent his righthand man and partner Isaac T. Mann down to look at the Saginaw forest. On June 6, 1898 all of the Camp Brothers' property was sold to Ritter and his associates for the sum of $12,000 at public auction.

The following year, Isaac T. Mann and William M. Ritter incorporated the Linville River Railway in Mitchell County, North Carolina as successor to the Camps' ill-fated line. The road was projected from the East Tennessee & Western North Carolina's end of track at Cranberry to Pineola, some 14 miles and the capital stock was set at $60,000. The charter for the new line stated that it would commence at or near Cranberry and "thence as said railroad is now located to a point at or near Pineola," an obvious reference to the Camp's efforts to build a logging railroad.

All of the stock of the Linville River railway was owned by W.M. Ritter Lumber Company men and the incorporators were, in addition to Ritter and Isaac Mann, Edwin Mann of Bluefield, West Virginia, James L. Harrell of Welch, West Virginia, W.B. Council of Boone, N.C. and J.B. Perry from Bramwell, West Virginia.

On April 28, 1899, the *Railway Gazette* reported that track laying had begun and was expected to be completed by the "middle of May." Ritter established an office at Pineola and work was begun on a new band mill. The former Camp brothers' circle sawmill was used to cut crossties, bridge timbers and lumber for the new band mill. Some timber was "Splash dammed" down the Linville River. Splash damming was used when the supply of water in a creek or river was not sufficient for a full scale river drive, or when the river was too rocky for the logs to float downstream under normal conditions. The loggers would store the timber in a large backed-up body of water and then release the water all at once, thus "driving" their logs downstream in the tide of newly released water. Splash damming enjoyed some popularity among the Appalachian loggers before the advent of the logging railroad, but at best it was a poor and wasteful means of getting the logs out of the hills.

As soon as the 33-pound rails of the Linville River Railway were in place as far as Pineola, the crews began laying tracks into the mountains. Eventually the trackage was quite extensive, snaking out of Pineola in five directions. To provide motive power for the Linville River railway as well as the extensive network of three-foot gauge logging trackage, Ritter brought in several locomotives from other logging operations, which were at that time largely centered in West Virginia. Ritter's logging activities eventually spread to the entire intermountain south as well as the coastal swamps in a search for more lumber. In use out of Pineola were an 0-6-0T called "Doodlebug," a large Class B Climax named "Old Grandmother" and a small Class "A" Climax that was sent to another Ritter operation in West Virginia in 1907, when a new two truck Shay arrived to handle the Linville River road assignments. Over the years, logging tracks were thrown down across Red Bird Gap to Jonas Ridge and to Pine Bottom, Crossnore, Altamont, Mill Timber Creek, Wilson Creek and down the Linville River as far as Linville Falls. One by one the areas were cut for their white pine, hemlock and spruce (tamarack). Log trains also operated over the Linville River Railway's tracks from Newland, where timber was cut on Kentucky Creek and Sugar Mountain.

To provide passenger service on the Linville River Railway, Ritter sent an old coach to the road and it was lettered Number 1. Freight equipment consisted of 10 flatcars and four boxcars, plus a number of log cars that were owned by the lumber company.

In 1906, the Ritter mill at Pineola cut most of the nearby timber. That summer, a narrow gauge line was constructed up Tiger Creek, south of Hampton,

Tennessee on the East Tennessee & Western North Carolina. A small mill was constructed near Hampton in 1910, and a third rail was laid on the ET&WNC from Elizabethton to Hampton, so that the Ritter lumber could be shipped out aboard standard gauge cars. The engines at Pineola were brought over to the Tiger Creek operation. By 1910 the line out of Hampton extended 12 miles and was being operated with four engines and 24 log cars. A commissary was built for the employees and a telephone line connected the mill with the logging camp. Back in the woods, a Lidgerwood skidder and a McGiffert log loader were in use.

The East Tennessee & Western North Carolina Railroad had begun to lay a third rail from Johnson City to Elizabethton (9.5 miles) in May, 1904. The job was finished in December, 1906, when work was then started to extend the third rail to the new Ritter operation at Hampton. It was necessary to widen the tunnel just west of Hampton in order to accommodate standard gauge cars. Narrow gauge engines handled all of the loads over the "bi-focal" line. When the ET&WNC converted their equipment from link and pin couplers in late 1903, the coupler height was raised so that it was the same as those on standard gauge cars. An ingenious swivel casting on the locomotive's pilot beam enabled the coupler to be swung over to the center line of standard gauge cars, or to be aligned with the narrow gauge equipment.

Bad Day on Banjo Branch

In 1907, the W.M. Ritter Lumber Company's big new three-foot gauge Shay, purchased only recently from the Lima Works, was heading east from Cranberry with the Linville River Railway daily mixed train for Pineola. Joe Powell the engineer and Homer Smithdeal the fireman had been doing a little drinking and they managed to turn the shiny Shay over into the Banjo Branch of the Toe River near Newland. The tipsy engine crew pulled themselves out of the water and sent a message to the office in Pineola for help, stating that the mixed train had gone astray. The mill switcher, a small Baldwin 0-6-0T, was dispatched to the scene of the wreck, but just as she was leaving town in a cloud of smoke, she broke a main-pin and coasted helplessly back to the yard on one cylinder. Word was then sent out to the woods crew to bring in their engine. The woods engine was a two truck Climax and as "Old Grandmother" was coming out of the woods, she hit a trestle across Harper's Creek and fell through the structure, killing engineer Ebb Smith and wrecking the engine. A call was then sent out to the ET&WNC, which loaned them their 24-ton Baldwin 2-6-0 Number 2 with Sherman Pippin as engineer. Sherman ran the little mogul on the Linville River Railway for 15 days until the logging line could get their engines picked up and repaired again.

By 1912, the Pineola mill had exhausted most of the readily available timber and the Ritter loggers began looking elsewhere for lumber. Since shortly after the turn of the century, Ritter had operated a mill at Mortimer, North Carolina and was busy cutting a large stand of timber north of Edgemont on the Carolina & Northwestern line (formerly Caldwell & Northern). Ritter's narrow gauge tracks radiated in three directions from Edgemont and one line up Lost Cove Creek was within a few miles of a spur line out of Pineola. It was a relatively simple matter to connect the two railroads and haul out all of the equipment, mill and all, over the Lost Cove Creek line, pulling up the tracks after the move. Operations out of Mortimer continued for another decade.

With the major timber holdings of the W.M. Ritter Lumber Company around Pineola having been cut-over, the Linville River Railway was of little importance to the lumbering firm. On August 1, 1913 the East Tennessee & Western North Carolina Railroad purchased the Linville River Railway and sent Charles (Cy) Grover Crumley over to rebuild the 12 miles of narrow gauge between the Cranberry Mine and Pineola. When Cy arrived in Pineola, he found things in deplorable condition. The light rails were badly worn and most of the crossties would have to be replaced before ET&WNC equipment could be run over the road. Equipment at that time on the Linville River line consisted of Number 1 Shay, Number 3 Climax, Number 1 coach, four boxcars and ten flats, all in a poor state of repair. Cy Crumley set about rebuilding the Linville River with 50 pound rail and new ties, using the Shay until he could get the line in shape for the heavier rod engines of the ET&WNC. The Climax engine was not used at all and by the following year, the Linville River Railway was being operated with equipment from the larger road. The Linville River's old cars and engines were then sold to a lumber company.

In the fall of 1913, long time Appalachian logger William S. Whiting purchased 2,600 acres of timber at Shulls Mills, North Carolina from the Lenoir Lumber Company and two years later, in May of 1915, he formed the Boone Fork Lumber Company to develop this stand of timber. Whiting and his brother Frank had operated lumber mills since 1892 when they began with a half interest in a single band sawmill on the Catawba River near Hickory, North Carolina. The Whiting Lumber Company was formed in 1897 and a large hardwood sawmill was constructed at Elizabethton, Tennessee on the East Tennessee & Western North Carolina. The Elizabethton plant was closed in 1904. Whiting then formed the Whiting Manufacturing Company and built a single band mill, planing mill and flooring mill at Abingdon, Virginia. He then began to log a number of tracts in Tennessee and North Carolina. Whiting used logging railroads to reach his timber and acquired a number of narrow gauge Climax locomotives for this work. His narrow gauge log cars were hauled over the logging railroad to a point between Laurel Bloomery and Mountain City, Tennessee, where the cars were turned over to the Laurel Railway for the haul to Laureldale, Virginia. They were then transferred to standard gauge cars (the narrow gauge cars were simply rolled aboard standard gauge flatcars with rails) for the rest of the trip to the Abingdon mill.

After extensive timber dealings in western North Carolina, including over 93,000 acres in Graham County, Whiting was ready to start logging the Shulls Mills timber. First, he would need a way to get his finished lumber to market and he approached the management of the ET&WNC in order to get their recently acquired Linville River Railway extended to the Boone Fork Lumber Company's millsite at Shulls Mills.

On June 30, 1915 the Board of Directors of the East Tennessee & Western North Carolina met in Philadelphia to approve an amendment to the charter of the Linville River Railway that would allow the road to be extended "to such points as determined by the board of directors." The stockholders approved the plan on July 14th and work was begun on the extension, with Cy Crumley again in charge of construction. The new line would be some 14 miles in length and would leave the original Linville River just south of Montezuma once known as Bull Scrape. ET&WNC locomotives 4, 5 and 6 were used in construction of the line, following the graders with ties, spikes and rails. In the meantime, the Boone Fork Lumber Company's new mill was going up at Shulls Mills. In order to obtain an unspecified bonus, the line was rushed to the mill site by September 25, 1916.

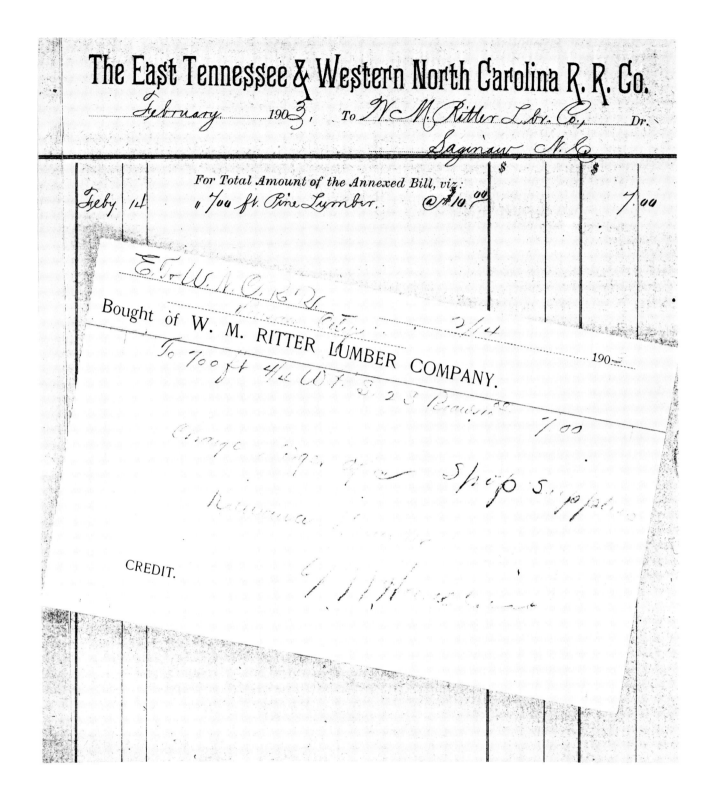

The East Tennessee & Western North Carolina R. R. Co.

February 190_3_, To _W. M. Ritter Lbr. Co.,_ Dr.

Saginaw, N. C.

| | | For Total Amount of the Annexed Bill, viz: | | $ | $ |
| Feby | 14 | " 700 ft. Pine Lumber. @ $10.00 | | | 7.00 |

E. T. & W. N. C. R R

Bought of W. M. RITTER LUMBER COMPANY.

190—

To 700 ft. 4/4 W. P. S. 2 S. Rough 7.00

CREDIT.

The lumber town of Pineola, on the Linville River Railway, was still known by its old
name of Saginaw on this 1903 waybill. W. M. Ritter operated an extensive network of logging railroads from the mill there.

In 1913, the Linville River line was sold to the ET&WNC. Cy Crumley (above right) was sent over to rebuild the old logging railroad from Cranberry to Pineola. Here a work train fills one of the many wooded trestles. — Cy Crumley from Ed Bond.

1914	175

East Tennessee & Western North Carolina R. R. Co.

PASS MR. H. P. FOXHALL,
ACCOUNT Supt., East Carolina Ry.

BETWEEN ALL STATIONS.
UNTIL DECEMBER 31ST, 1914 { UNLESS OTHERWISE ORDERED AND
{ SUBJECT TO CONDITIONS ON BACK

PRESIDENT.

GIBBS-INMAN CO LOUISVILLE

The lumber company began construction of their own three-foot gauge logging railroad and acquired more standing timber on the slopes of Grandfather Mountain from the Linville Improvement Company. Tracks were thrown up Moody Mill Creek and into the upper reaches of Boone Fork Creek and Pilot Ridge, under the shadow of the famous old mountain and tourist mecca. By 1917, more than 300 men were working at Shulls Mills, cutting spruce, poplar, ash, oak, chestnut and other hardwoods. Pulpwood was shipped to the Champion Fibre Company of Canton, North Carolina, which had its own network of logging roads in the Appalachians. In service on the Boone Fork Lumber Company's six miles of trackage were several Shays and a Class A Climax, locally known as a "Black Satchel."

The lumber company constructed a hotel at Shulls Mills. If it had a formal name, it was soon discarded, for lumbermen referred to the frame Victorian structure as the "Blue Goose Hotel," a reflection on the poor heating provided by a pot-bellied stove located on each floor.

In 1920, the Boone Fork Lumber Company purchased a new Climax locomotive and ten new logging cars from the Kilby Car Company to bring in timber from Howard Creek and Buckeye Gap near Rich Mountain. The Climax engine arrived in Johnson City, was set up and a full head of steam built in its boiler. Long time engineer Frank M. Allison and his fireman—son C. C. "Brownie" Allison were called out to run the new engine behind the passenger train to Shulls Mills. Leaving long after the passenger train had departed, the Boone Fork Lumber Company Climax soon caught up with the regular train and followed it into the sawmill town.

Linville River Extension

With the end of track only eight miles away, the citizens of Boone, North Carolina caught a bad case of "railroad fever." Led by Doctor B. B. Dougherty of the Appalachian State Teacher's College, the townspeople of Boone voted a $27,000 bond issue to entice the Linville River Railway to extend its tracks. Rob Rivers, editor of the *Watauga Democrat*, ran editorials in his paper urging passage of the bond issue and the people approved the measure on February 12, 1918. Chief Engineer Dyer of the East Tennessee & Western North Carolina R.R. laid out the route and the first earth was broken at Boone on the afternoon of March 7th At Shulls Mills, lumbering continued. The mill was cutting 65,000 feet of lumber each day and had four and a half million feet in the drying yards.

By March 21, 1918, over two hundred men were employed on the new line and a large number of teams were working toward Boone, as the grade was thrown across the farms of A. D. Blair, E. S. Coffey and G. C. Winkler. The oldest employee was Captain William H. Hodges, who was eighty-six. Some rock work was necessary at the high cliff on the Watauga River and the 300-foot hillside cut was finished on April 11th. Ten days later the grade was finished to near the depot site, where a wye was being graded. Grading was supervised by Joe H. Wagner and his brother Herb. Crossties were cut from native oak on the Winkler Farm and the railroad purchased a small sawmill from W. L. Haynes and moved it to the Winkler tract on June 6th. As soon as the grade was ready, Cy Crumley brought up his construction train with loads of rail and track hardware for the track gangs. Track was laid to Holler's Mill by late June and by August 8, 1918, the grade past Hodges Gap, into Boone was completed. By early October the rails had been spiked in place through the Gap and were within "whistle sound" of Boone. The first construction train with 2-8-0 Number 4 arrived in Boone on October 24, 1918. Local farmers could now ship cabbage and potatoes over the new line.

The year is 1914 and a varnish run waits at the Pineola Depot. On the rear of the Linville River train is the ET&WNC's parlor car "Azalea." The Linville River Railway has just been taken-over and rebuilt by the ET&WNC. Conductor Cy Crumley and brakemen Holtsclaw and McCurry wait for the scheduled departure over LR-ET&WNC tracks to Johnson City. At Montezuma Junction, (below) the tracks lead off toward Linville, while the curved rails head to Pineola. — William S. Cannon.

Cy Crumley's crew was busy laying out the Boone Yards and wye the week before Christmas and mail service was established between Johnson City and Boone on January 1, 1919. Regular passenger service over the new road was inaugurated on Saturday, May 9, 1919 at 4:00 p.m. with Cy Crumley as conductor. Timetable Number 83 (May 8, 1919) shows through train service from Tennessee to Boone. The train was scheduled to arrive at 4:00 p.m. and depart Boone the next morning at 6:30 a.m. The entire town turned out to see the steam train come puffing into Boone that nice May afternoon. A number of speeches were made welcoming the railroad and the long-winded local politicos heaped praise upon the slim rails and promised a new era for the citizens of the backwoods country. However it was Mayor J. H. Shull from over Banner Elk way that summed it all up when he said "I remember when the only way a person could get to Boone was to be born there," then he sat down! *Watauga Democrat* Editor Rivers and the whole town agreed it was the shortest and best speech they had ever heard. Mrs. C. W. Gunlock wrote a poem for the occasion:

Leaving Boone

I'm going on the narrow gauge.
That is the train for me.
It will take you to Johnson City.
That is in Tennessee.

The depot was finished and an extension made to the wye track. Farmer B. Blackburn had to have part of his barn cut away in order to provide the extra room for the wye's tail track. R. R. Johnson was named as the first agent at Boone. Special trains were run and weekend picnic specials were the social events of the town. Agent Johnson moved into his office in the new depot on September 11th and by this time a daily freight was scheduled to leave town at 8:00 a.m. and return at 4:30 p.m. The winter schedule saw a mixed train to Cranberry at 6:30 a.m., returning the following day at 5:30 p.m.

James Connelly Moore used the Linville River trains to string a power line that brought electric lights to Boone and ET&WNC General Superintendent Frank Allison donated a carload of crushed rock from the Cranberry Mine in order to pave the sidewalk from the depot to the Critcher Hotel. Local folks figured Boone was "living high on the hog" with the arrival of the Linville River Railroad.

Shortly after the line to Boone was completed and before the tracks had been put in shape, Engineer Sherman Pippin left Boone at 6:40 one morning with a combination RPO-Express car, two coaches and the "Azalea." The parlor car was the pride and joy of the combined East Tennessee & Western North Carolina and Linville River Railroads. It had been raining for several days and a flash flood had weakened a high fill on the heavy grade between Shulls Mills and Linville. As Train Number 1 started across the fill, the trim 4-6-0 began to tilt as the fill gave way. Sherman made it to the far side and brought the train to a halt with the combination car hanging across the gap, supported only by the rails and the strain on its own couplers. Conductor Cy Crumley was following the regular train with a work train and arrived at the scene with engine #4 some ten minutes later. Cy placed a pole up against the side of the Railway Post Office car Number 15 and put some ties against the engine's right side to keep it from tilting over. The crews then built up under the tracks, placing a temporary crosstie bridge under the sagging rails. This required over four hours of working under the train, which could have fallen into the gap at any moment. Finally the Number 4 engine eased the three rear cars back off the fill as Cy uncoupled them from the RPO car. Engineer Sherman Pippin and fireman Lorne Harrison then eased the combination car off the fill and everyone took a deep breath. No one was injured and damage was very slight. The event made Ripley's "Believe It Or Not" in newspapers all across the country.

Train Time at Cranberry

ET&WNC No. 9 gets ready to leave the Cranberry depot (above) and charge up the switchback to the mainline. — J. T. Dowdy, Ed Bond Coll. At upper left, the Linville River crew stands beside their combine. Number 6 waits at the Cranberry scales in 1909 with a lumber train. Her crew is Walter R. Allison (in cab), Jim Livingston, Bill Lewis, Carson Salyer, Fuse Jenkins and Charlie Archer.

Cranberry's depot was located in the valley below the mine and was reached via a switchback from the mainline. Ten-wheeler Number 9 waits to pull out (above) in 1923. The depot (below) was located near the Cranberry Iron & Coal Company store and the covered car shed. The mainline can be seen on the hillside. — J. T. Dowdy Coll. from Ed Bond.

The joint ET&WNC-LR passenger depot at Cranberry (above) served also as the Western Union office and in later years as the town's post office. An excursion train (below) has just arrived at Cranberry. The year is 1920 and the train is trailed by three specially-built excursion cars. — J. T. Dowdy Coll. from Ed Bond.

East Tennessee & Western North Carolina
RAILROAD CO.

✳ *CLERICAL TICKET* ✳ **1916**
On presentation of this check

NOT TRANSFERABLE

Rev....

of..
Is entitled to MINISTERIAL RATES for himself only, subject to the
conditions printed on the back of this until **December 31st, 1916.**

No. **E**..
Vice-Pres't and Supt.

The ET&WNC and LR lines ran through the heart of the "Bible Belt" and so it was not unusual for them to issue passes for free transportation to members of the clergy. ET&WNC Superintendent Hardin would not allow trains to run on Sundays for many years. A baptism takes place (above) in Cranberry Creek, below the Linville River's engine-house. It is still a common sight in Tweetsie Country to see hardshell sayings painted on rocks. — Drawing by Mike Pearsall.

The ET&WNC and LR lines had their share of wrecks, washouts and derailments. Ten-wheeler Number 8 derailed her tender (above) on the Cranberry Wye in 1912. — Ed Bond Coll. The 10 spot had her problems with a split switch at Newland's West switch. Props kept her upright until the wrecking crew arrived. — William S. Cannon Coll.

Train No. 2 — Late Today

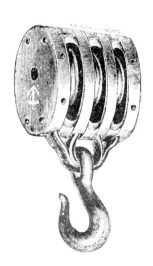

41

The first train to reach Boone, North Carolina signaled the start of a big celebration. Mayor Shull from Banner Elk said on the occasion: "I remember when the only way a person could get to Boone was to be born there." Trains are shown at the new depot (above) shortly after regular service was begun on May 9, 1919. Engine #11, at right, heads a three car train, while another ten-wheeler waits with her consist by the station. — J. T. Dowdy Coll. from Ed Bond. **Old-timers in the hill country recall an old folk dance to the tune of a five-string banjo.** — State of Tennessee photo, drawing by Mike Pearsall.

First Train to Boone

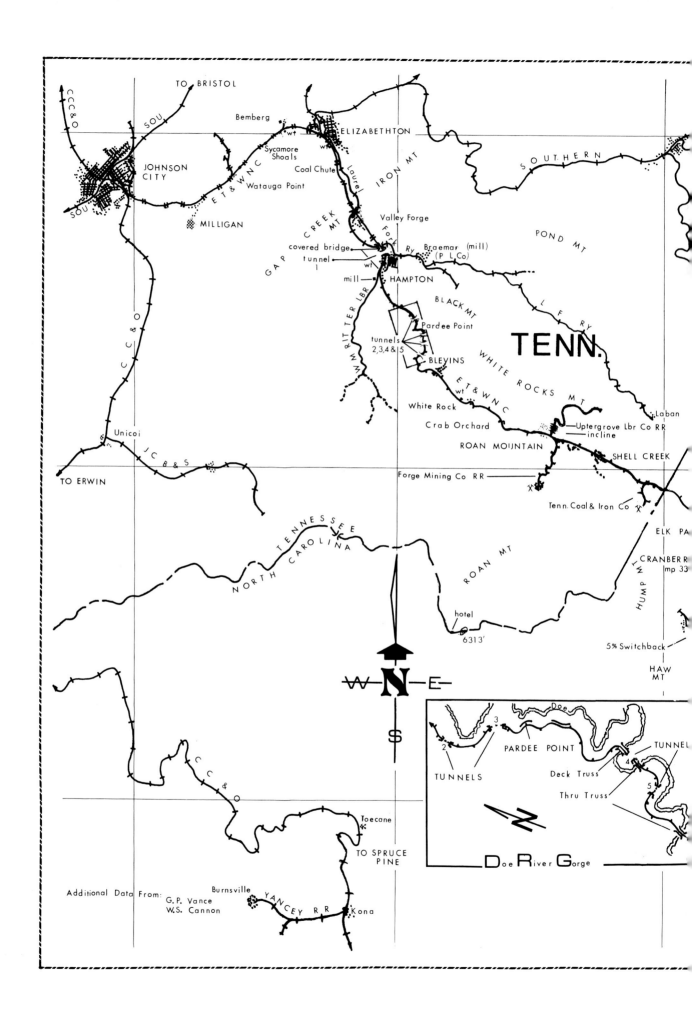

TO BRISTOL

CC&O

SOU

Bemberg

ELIZABETHTON

JOHNSON
CITY

Sycamore
Shoals

wt

Coal Chute

ET&WNC

Watauga Point

Laurel

IRON MT

SOUTHERN

SOU

MILLIGAN

GAP
CREEK
MT

Valley Forge

POND MT

covered bridge

tunnel
1

wt

Ry

Braemar (mill)
(P L Co)

mill

HAMPTON

BLACK MT

L F RY

CC&O

M RITTER LBR

Pardee Point

tunnels
2,3,4 & 5

TENN.

BLEVINS

WHITE ROCKS MT

wt

ET&WNC

White Rock

Laban

Crab Orchard

Uptergrove Lbr Co RR

incline

Unicoi

JC B&S

ROAN MOUNTAIN

SHELL CREEK

TO ERWIN

Forge Mining Co RR

Tenn. Coal & Iron Co

ELK PA

NORTH TENNESSEE

CAROLINA

ROAN MT

HUMP MT

CRANBER R
mp 33

hotel

6313'

5% Switchback

HAW
MT

W N E

S

CC&O

Toecane

TO SPRUCE
PINE

Additional Data From:
    G. P. Vance
    W. S. Cannon

Burnsville

YANCEY R R

Kona

Doe

PARDEE POINT

TUNNEL

3

2

TUNNELS

Deck Truss

4

Thru Truss

5

N

Doe River Gorge

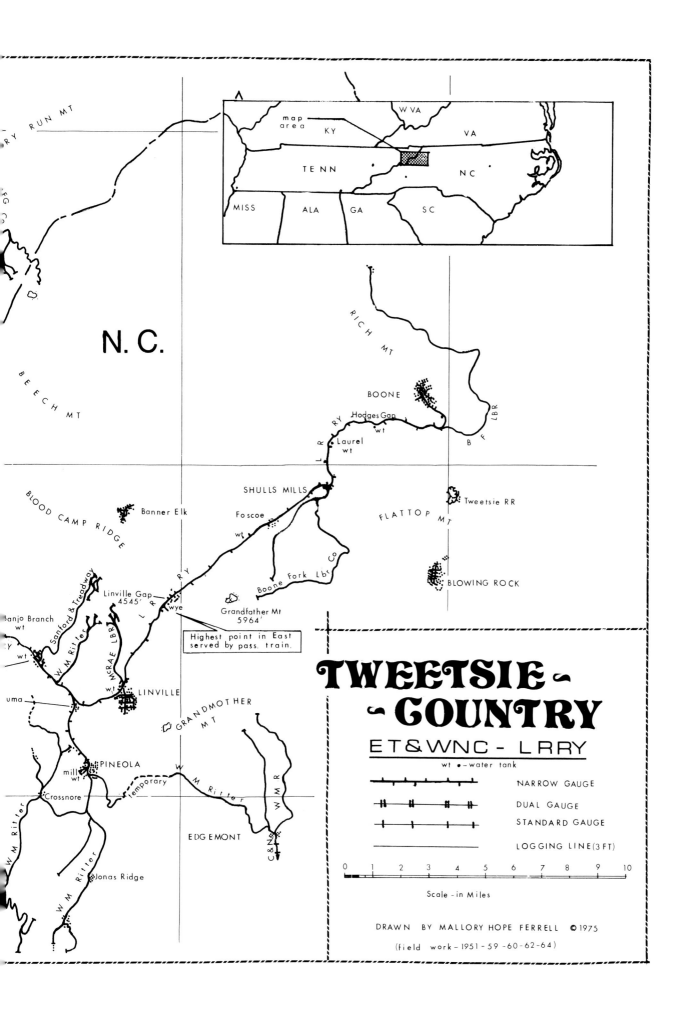

N.C.

RICH MT

BOONE

Hodges Gap
wt

Laurel
wt

BEECH MT

BLOOD CAMP RIDGE

SHULLS MILLS

Banner Elk

Foscoe

wt

Tweetsie RR

FLATTOP MT

Boone Fork Lbr

Co

BLOWING ROCK

Linville Gap
4545'

wye

Grandfather Mt
5964'

Highest point in East
served by pass. train.

Banjo Branch
wt

Sanford & Treadway

W M Ritter

McRAE LBR

wt   LINVILLE

GRANDMOTHER
MT

uma

mill
wt   PINEOLA

Crossnore

temporary

W M Ritter

W M R

W M Ritter

EDGEMONT

C&N

Jonas Ridge

W M Ritter

TWEETSIE ~
~ COUNTRY
ET&WNC - LRRY

wt • — water tank

NARROW GAUGE

DUAL GAUGE

STANDARD GAUGE

LOGGING LINE (3 FT)

0   1   2   3   4   5   6   7   8   9   10

Scale - in Miles

DRAWN BY MALLORY HOPE FERRELL   © 1975

(field work – 1951 – 59 – 60 – 62 – 64)

map
area   KY

W VA

VA

TENN

NC

MISS   ALA   GA   SC

Pat. Jan. 31, June 13, 1893, by Wm. H. Campbell, Brooklyn, N. Y.

Linville River Railway Co.

Conductor's Receipt.

Conductors must give one of these receipts for every cash fare collected.

This part is of NO VALUE except as a receipt for the amount paid, and is good for this day and train only.

Passengers will notice that the lower LARGE figures show the full amount paid to the Conductor; if not, please notify

Form C. R.   *Geo. W. Hardin.*
                                            Superintendent.

2857

Amount of Fare Collected.

05 FIVE CENTS	
10 TEN CENTS	05 Five Cents
15 FIFTEEN CENTS	10 Ten Cents
20 TWENTY CENTS	15 Fifteen Cents
25 TWENTY-FIVE CENTS	20 Twenty Cents
30 THIRTY CENTS	25 Twenty-five Cents
35 THIRTY-FIVE CENTS	30 Thirty Cents
40 FORTY CENTS	35 Thirty-five Cents
45 FORTY-FIVE CENTS	40 Forty Cents
50 FIFTY CENTS	45 Forty-five Cents
55 FIFTY-FIVE CENTS	50 Fifty Cents
60 SIXTY CENTS	55 Fifty-five Cents
65 SIXTY-FIVE CENTS	60 Sixty Cents
70 SEVENTY CENTS	65 Sixty-five Cents
75 SEVENTY-FIVE CENTS	70 Seventy Cents
80 EIGHTY CENTS	75 Seventy-five Cents
85 EIGHTY-FIVE CENTS	80 Eighty Cents
90 NINETY CENTS	85 Eighty-five Cents
95 NINETY-FIVE CENTS	90 Ninety Cents
1.00 ONE DOLLAR	95 Ninety-five Cents
1.05 DOLLAR FIVE	1.00 One Dollar
1.10 DOLLAR TEN	1.05 Dollar Five
1.15 DOLLAR FIFTEEN	1.10 Dollar Ten
1.20 DOLLAR TWENTY	1.15 Dollar Fifteen
1.25 DOLLAR TWENTY-FIVE	1.20 Dollar Twenty
1.30 DOLLAR THIRTY	1.25 Dollar Twenty-five
1.35 DOLLAR THIRTY-FIVE	1.30 Dollar Thirty
	1.35 Dollar Thirty-five

Throughout the narrow gauge days of the ET&WNC and LR lines, Cy Crumley was one of the best loved and most colorful employees. Cy is shown (below, opposite) beside the Number 4 at Shulls Mills in 1920. — Ed Bond Coll. Shortly after the line to Boone was opened in 1919, Engineer Sherman Pippin was taking the morning varnish run out of Boone when he hit a washed-out fill near Shulls Mills. The train came to a halt suspended over the fill (above). Conductor Crumley arrived with a work train and placed a pole against the tilting RPO-Express car. The event made Ripley's "Believe It Or Not" in newspapers across the country. — R. W. Richardson Coll.

If Clergy put No. of Permit here.	VOID AFTER	JAN FEB	MAR APR	MAY JUN	JUL AUG	SEP OCT	NOV DEC	Day 1	3	5	7	9	11	13	15	17	19	21	23	25	27	29	31	1926	1927	1928	1929	1930	1931
								2	4	6	8	10	12	14	16	18	20	22	24	26	28	30							

Linville River Railway Company

One First Class Continuous Passage unless otherwise canceled.

Punch here ★ for Baggage

Form D. L. 2.

CRANBERRY to Station Opposite Point in Margin below.

GOOD FOR ONE FIRST CLASS CONTINUOUS PASSAGE only on trains stopping at destination. Void after midnight of date canceled by "L" punch in margin above. VOID IF IT SHOWS ANY ALTERATIONS, ERASURES, OR IS MUTILATED IN ANY MANNER, or if B. C. PUNCH is in any other than place DESIGNATED. IF MORE THAN ONE DATE, DESTINATION OR CLASS IS CANCELED, it will only be accepted within the shortest limit, to the shortest destination, for the lowest class canceled. If "CLERGY" it will be good only when accompanied by Clergy Permit. Baggage liability limited to wearing apparel not exceeding $100 in value. The right is reserved by this Company to check baggage to final destination only.

NO STOP-OVER ALLOWED.

J.C. Vance
Vice President.

25853

★	★	N.C		N.C	N.C	N.C	N.C	N.C	N.C	N.C	N. C	N.C	N.C	N.C	N.C	N.C	N.C	★	CLASS		
★	★																	★	CHARITY		
★	★	Cranberry	Minneapolis	VALE	NEWLAND	Montezuma	PINEOLA	LINVILLE	Linville Gap	JestesSiding	Townsend	FOSCOE	Shulls Mills	LAUREL	Hodge'sGap	BOONE		★	SPECIAL		
★	★																	★	HALF		
★	★																	★	CLERGY		
★	★	CRANBERRY	MINNEAPOLIS	VALE	NEWLAND	MONTEZUMA	PINEOLA	LINVILLE	LINVILLE GAP	JESTES SIDING	TOWNSEND	FOSCOE	SHULLS MILLS	LAUREL	HODGE'S GAP	BOONE		★	CHARITY	SPECIAL	HALF CLERGY
★	★	N.C	N.C	N.C	N.C	N.C	N.C	N.C	N. C	N.C	N.C	N.C	N.C	N.C	N.C	N.C		★	CLASS		

Linville River Railway Company

"DREWRY TICKET"

AGENT'S STUB—Not Good for Passage.

CRANBERRY to Station Named in Margin above.

If Clergy put No. of Permit here.

RATE $

Issued_____19___   Via_____

Expires _____19___

25853

FORM D. L. 2

48

Linville depot, located near Linville Gap, was a rustic shingle-covered building that served the tourist who annually came to spend the summer months at nearby cabins and resorts. Period autos date the 1921 scene, above. — Earl Hardy from Hugh Morton Coll. **Number 9** leads a three car train (opposite, top). Behind lies Linville Gap, at 4,545 feet above sea level, the highest point in the Eastern United States served by a passenger train.

Linville Depot

49

ET&WNC Number 14 pauses with her crew at the Newland depot (opposite, top) during World War I. Fireman Brownie Allison, Engineer Charles Miller, trainmen Still Oakes (in cab) and Grover Miller stand beside the 4-6-0 along with agent Nat Fletcher. — William S. Cannon Coll. Conductor Cy Crumley is shown in a 1913 view inside the Newland depot. (opposite, lower) Engine Number 6 has been bucking snow in the view (above) at Newland, taken in 1914. Her crew this day is Paul Fletcher, fireman; Grover Miller, brakeman; Claude Simerly, trainman; Cy Crumley, conductor; Charlie Miller, engineer and Paul Cooper, brakeman.

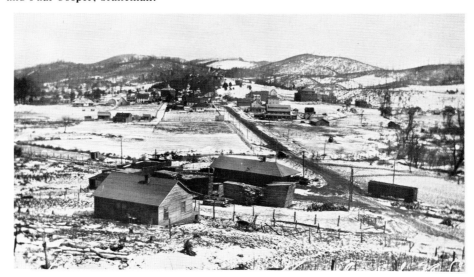

The Cranberry Engine House

In the early 1900's the Cranberry shops (above) were busy with the engines of the ET&WNC, LR and Cranberry Iron's own 0-4-0T (top). — Ed Bond Coll. Stub switches lead into the house in the 1941 view by Robert B. Adams (opposite, top). The 12 stops for water, beside the car shed in a 1942 R. W. Richardson print. (lower)

52

Hauling a string of new vestibule passenger cars through the Doe River Gorge, the East Tennessee & Western North Carolina-Linville River train was classed as the finest on any American narrow gauge road. — Hugh Morton Coll.

54

4

Riding the Stemwinder

With over sixty-five miles of mainline in operation between Johnson City and Boone, the East Tennessee & Western North Carolina Railroad and its Linville River Railway began to assume the appearance of a mainline carrier by the summer of 1919.

The narrow gauge had slowly added to its stable of iron horses, acquiring new Baldwin consolidation engines in 1902, 1903 and 1904. In 1906, a Brooks built 0-8-0 switcher was ordered and when it was delivered in mid-summer the new engine was hailed as the largest narrow gauge engine of her day. In 1907, the ET&WNC began buying Baldwin ten wheelers and by 1919 had acquired seven of them. The 4-6-0's seemed perfectly suited to the operating conditions found on the ET&WNC-LR lines and served for over three decades.

The East Tennessee & Western North Carolina and Linville River took on mainline proportions with the acquisition of a number of vestibule-equipped passenger cars which were built by the Jackson & Sharp Works between 1917 and 1921. The ET&WNC-LR varnish run was trailed by a beautiful, brass railed Parlor Car named the "Azalea." The cars were painted Pullman Green and comprised the only narrow gauge, vestibuled passenger train in the United States at that time. The Denver & Rio Grande Western, in distant Colorado later added rebuilt vestibule cars to its passenger trains on the narrow gauge runs between Alamosa and Durango and between Salida and Montrose.

The ET&WNC-LR passenger run made quite a sight as the trim 4-6-0 hauled the daily express trains (Numbers 1 and 2) through the Doe River Gorge and past Pardee Point, trailing a consist of a combination mail-baggage-express and oval windowed coaches fresh from the Delaware car maker. Those desiring to ride aboard the Parlor Car paid an additional fifty cents, but the view from the rear platform of the "Azalea" was well worth the price. The management provided wicker chairs and a red and white canvas awning for those desiring to ride on the open platform in order to gaze out on the less fortunate as the train worked up the 4 percent grades and around the 32 degree curves.

While dining car and Pullman service was not provided, passengers could enjoy fine food at John Sevier's Hotel, just across the tracks from the ET&WNC's gingerbread station at Johnson City. Fine accommodations were also available at General John Wilder's Cloudland Hotel above Roan Mountain, Tennessee. After the Cloudland closed in 1915, passengers could dine and sleep at the Roan Mountain Inn. Eight miles from Elk Park by stage was the Klonteska Inn and Lowe's

Hotel at Banner Elk, North Carolina. The Esceola Inn at Linville was opened to ET&WNC-LR passengers in 1915, wen the three-foot gauge tracks reached that point and through parlor car service was initiated "daily except Sunday." The Victorian design of the Pineola Inn offered pleasant surroundings for the traveler at that point. At Montezuma, John and Sarah Jane Carpenter ran a ten room hotel in a two story building near the railroad. This hotel was noted for its good food and two beautiful daughters who served it .

From the earliest days, the East Tennessee & Western North Carolina Railroad ran excursion trains for those living along its tracks. In the autumn of 1903, just such a train was returning from a circus, when it stopped briefly on the high deck covered bridge just outside of Hampton, Tennessee. The train was made up of passenger cars and gondolas that had been converted for the occasion with planks for benches. One of the passengers, Bob Simerly, stepped off the train, not realizing that it was on the high bridge! He fell seventy feet down to the Doe River and hit with a splash in about two feet of water. The train crew, headed by engineer Sherman Pippin, rushed down the steep, brush covered embankment, expecting to bring back a dead body. They were met about two-thirds of the way down by a banged-up but laughing Bob Simerly, who was in pretty good shape considering the experience. His short flight attracted more attention in the hills thereabouts than did the flight of Orville and Wilbur Wright that same year on the sands of Kitty Hawk.

In 1911 two special excursion cars were built in the Johnson City shops and in 1917, another pair of the open excursion cars were added to the roster. Tourism was becoming an economic factor in the operations of the line. Already scores of wealthy "flatlanders" were discovering the beauty of the Linville and Grandfather Mountain area and mountain estates were being built near the Linville River and in the Gap. Golf courses and resorts were built along the Linville River Railway, notably at Pineola and Linville.

Avery County was formed in 1911 from parts of Mitchell, Caldwell and Watauga Counties. The settlement at Old Fields of Toe was renamed Newland and became the county seat. By this time folks were no longer calling the nearby settlement Bull Scrape; it acquired a new name: Montezuma.

Nat Fletcher was the agent at Newland, North Carolina. In later years, economy measures forced a cut-back of employees and Nat took over the duties at Linville, too. Fletcher would sell tickets, check baggage and direct the passengers to the train and after all the L.C.L. (Less Car Load) freight was aboard the combine and the train had pulled out of the station, Nat would jump in his "Whippet" automobile and drive like crazy down the dirt road to Linville. The travelers, upon arriving at Linville, would see the same depot agent they had just seen back at Newland. Since the train had to make a run down to Pineola between Newland and Linville, it is not likely that Nat Fletcher had to "floorboard" his tin lizzie.

The Blue Ridge Mountains, like New England, was covered bridge country. The rustic wooden structures once dotted the countryside and provided both a picturesque and unitarian means by which the hill people could get their products to market. To this day a beautiful, white framed covered bridge, built in 1882, carries traffic across the Doe River in Elizabethton, not far from the ET&WNC tracks. Covered bridges also provided a means by which the narrow gauge tracks crossed the Doe and Little Doe Rivers near Hampton, Tennessee. The most unique covered bridge was a deck type, three span, Howe truss bridge just west of Hampton. The deck truss sat on native stone abutments and was 289 feet long. Built in 1882, the barn red structure carried trains of the ET&WNC from the first to the

56

The trains of the ET&WNC-LR passed through the heart of the Blue Ridge Mountains on their daily runs between Johnson City in Tennessee and Boone, over in North Carolina. The daily train is shown at speed (above) in a view from the J. T. Dowdy Collection. — From Ed Bond. A typical sight from the open windows is shown below.

last. Old timers also recall another covered bridge across the Doe at Blevins, east of the last tunnel, but it was replaced in 1909 with an iron bridge. A covered bridge at Shell Creek was also replaced with an iron structure at this time.

Just east of Hampton was another covered bridge, this one a conventional Howe through truss bridge across the Little Doe River at mile post 14.71. This bridge was also built in 1882 and served the railroad throughout its lifetime. This covered bridge was a single span affair and was 118 feet, 8 inches long.

Sherman Pipin, one of the line's more colorful engineers, was running a passenger train with engine Number 2, a Baldwin 2-6-0, in the early days on the run from Johnson City to Cranberry. For several weeks there had been talk that birds had built a nest in the little covered bridge east of Hampton and they should be cleaned out before sparks from a passing engine started a bad fire, but nothing had been done. Pippin came wheeling along with the varnish run and noticed that a previous train had set fire to one of the nests. Being a quick fellow, Sherm kept up his speed and put out the fire as the train passed by, using the wash-down hose. Somehow the superintendent, George W. Hardin, heard about what Pippin had done and "raised hell" with him, telling him that if the bridge had been burning harder when Pippin rolled through that the "company would have got lawed 'til hell froze-over!" In later years, Engineer Pippin remarked that Mr. Hardin was "hard in name and nature." The super notified all enginemen that in the future they were to stop and walk across any bridge or trestle that might be on fire.

Conductor Angel and the crew of Baldwin 2-8-0 Number 6 are shown on the Linville River in October 1923.

Engineer Sherman Pippin was quite a ladies gentleman in his day, too. He "went firing" with the East Tennessee & Western North Carolina Railroad in the 1890's, as soon as he was old enough and stayed with the road his entire working life, save for a few months he spent firing on the Baltimore & Ohio up in West Virginia. Pippin read the *Bible*, Shakespeare and Forney's *Catechism of the Locomotive* with equal enthusiasm and was adept at quoting any of them. One day, a young girl from Elizabethton passed a poem to the dashing engineer as he paused at the depot with the daily passenger train. Sixty years later, the poem was given the author by Mr. Pippin, then living in retirement on his farm near Roan Mountain.

> **Eva loves the railroad men.**
> **I think you will agree.**
> **And now I will tell you a story,**
> **As she has told to me.**
>
> **She first loved a conductor,**
> **Whose eyes were of deepest blue,**
> **Eva loved him dearly,**
> **But he was very untrue.**
>
> **But I guess he was not so awful mean,**
> **For every one have their faults.**
> **And if he didn't love her,**
> **You couldn't blame Tom Saults.**
>
> **One day she went to Cranberry,**
> **And everyone could see,**
> **That it wasn't Eva he was loving,**
> **But Josie Bradley.**
>
> **So Eva came back to Elizabethton,**
> **And when two Sundays come,**
> **Josie and Tom will marry,**
> **For she's feeding him on roses and plums.**
>
> **But they say that Eva's in love again,**
> **With somebody very dear,**
> **But it isn't a conductor this time,**
> **But a "Little Engineer."**

Sherman Pippin was active in the Brotherhood of Locomotive Engineers And Firemen and on one occasion, when the East Tennessee & Western North Carolina Railroad claimed it was losing money, he wrote to his congressman and obtained copies of the Interstate Commerce Commission (ICC) reports which showed the narrow gauge to be doing quite well. Confronting Superintendent Hardin with the reports, he got a raise for the enginmen. George W. Hardin was a firm, hard nosed brass hat who was set in his ways and for many years resisted running regular trains on Sundays. This was the "Bible Belt" of the Southland and it was not uncommon at all to see "Jesus Saves" painted on large rocks near sharp curves. Baptisms were often held just below the railroad's yards at Cranberry and men of the cloth were afforded free passes over the Stemwinder's tracks.

Normal operations, following completion of the Linville River Railway into Boone, North Carolina in 1918, saw the daily passenger train leave Johnson City at 1:00 p.m. as train Number 2. This run would begin with Sherman Pippin giving two short whistle bursts from the ten wheeler as the consist rolled through the streets

Engineer Sherman Pippin guides 4-6-0 Number 8 with the daily passenger train in about 1915. The train is typical for the period with an RPO-combine, two coaches and the parlor car "Azalea" on the rear. — Ed Bond Coll.

of Johnson City and out into the open countryside. The train would be made up of a combination baggage-mail-express car, several coaches and the parlor car "Azalea" on the rear. This car, with its bow-topped windows, stained glass clerestories, carpeted aisles and swivel arm chairs was the place to be when the train picked up speed and passed the shop area on three rail trackage. Standard gauge freight cars towered over the train and the engineer on the broad gauge Clinchfield 2-8-0 might look down upon the consist, but it was the finest narrow guage varnish run in the country and everybody knew it. After a brief pause at the frame depot in Elizabethton, Tennessee, the train was on its way into the hills. Dashing across the deck-type covered bridge and into a tunnel, Number 2 paused at Hampton to take on mail, experss, L.C.L. and local passengers. Up front in the combine, employees of the United States Post Office Department would be busy sorting mail for points up the line. With a couple of whistle blasts, Number 2 would be off again, pounding upgrade through another covered bridge and into the depths of the Doe River Gorge with its granite cliffs and many tunnels. After pausing at Roan Mountain, the train crossed into North Carolina and pulled into Elk Park, with its large frame depot and a sheet-tin roof overhang that provided locals with a fine, shaded vantage point to watch the goings on. Fireman Earl Vest would work at building up a head of steam on the 4-6-0, as the sleepy community came alive for a few minutes. After a short run, the train arrived at Cranberry and the mine that provided most of the ET&WNC's traffic. After a switch was thrown, the train would head down the switchback to the Cranberry depot, located in the meadow below. At 3:12 p.m. and after a brief stop at the depot, the train would whistle-off again, this time blasting up the grade of the switchback and onto the tracks of the Linville River Railway.

While equipment was lettered for either the East Tennessee & Western North Carolina or the Linville River, it was operated interchangeably. Some cars were transferred from one road to the other over the years, but following purchase of the Linville River line by the larger road, the numbering system for the two railroads was the same.

The daily passenger train reached Montezuma at 3:57 p.m. At 3,882 feet above sea level, it was the highest railroad depot in the eastern United States. Leaving the spot once known as Bull Scrape, the tracks circled Pegram's ice pond. During the winter months, ice was harvested here and stored in a large barn nearby for summer use. Montezuma was also noted for its high grade moonshine whiskey. After a short time the train backed down the line to Pineola, once the original mainline of the Linville River under W.M. Ritter Lumber Company ownership, but now a branch. Pineola was the home of many rich Easterners during the summer months and the Mormon family, builders of the Mormon Automobile, had a fine estate there. At 4:15, if the train were on schedule, Pippin would whistle off for Linville, dropping down through Ledford's pasture on the way to the summer cottages of the resort town.

The rustic Linville depot was located at mile post 46 and there was a water tank and a passing siding there. Mr. Yoder would come over from the post office to get the mail and Sheriff Hartley usually dropped by to see who was aboard the train. Esten Lambert would be waiting there with his wagon to pick up any passengers for the resort hotel or even distant Banner Elk. Shortly after the train left Linville, it crested the grade at Linville Gap, 4,545 feet above sea level, making it the highest point in the eastern half of the country served by a passenger train. In summer months, the air was full of the smell of galax and other mountain wild-flowers. Near Shulls Mills, the train would slow to a walking pace, for up ahead, a Climax geared locomotive of the Boone Fork Lumber Company would have the mainline temporarily blocked with a log train. Soon the logger would back into the mill and the ten-wheeler was again working hard up the grade to Hodges Gap. Boone, North Carolina came into sight a few minutes after six and the train would lay over there for the night. As Train Number 1, it would depart at 6:40 the next morning.

These were good days for the East Tennessee & Western North Carolina and Linville River lines, but all too soon, from far off New York City would come word of a stock market crash. Although this did not seem to bother anyone in the hills, since they did not own any stock, the implications were deeper than they at first appeared. Trouble lay ahead for the narrow gauge and the people she served.

Covered
Bridge
Country

The Blue Ridge Mountains were covered bridge country. The rustic structures once dotted the countryside and they served the ET&WNC as well. Number 12 heads out of a tunnel and onto the deck-type bridge just west of Hampton in 1938. — James P. Shuman. The same bridge is shown (opposite) — Lloyd D. Lewis Coll. The Roan Mountain bard was photographed by Jane C. Moore.

Mainstay Motive Power

The mainstay motive power for both the ET&WNC and LR were a fleet of Baldwin ten-wheelers. The first 4-6-0 arrived in 1907 and by 1919 the lines had acquired a stable. The 4-6-0's seemed perfectly suited to the operating conditions found on the ET&WNC-LR. The last of the ten-wheelers Number 14 (above) is shown at Johnson City in 1941. — G. P. Vance from Ed Bond Col. **Number 9 is shown in a Baldwin builder's photo.** — Herb Broadbelt Col. **The Number 12 (opposite, top) is shown at Johnson City in 1937.** — Lawrie Brown.

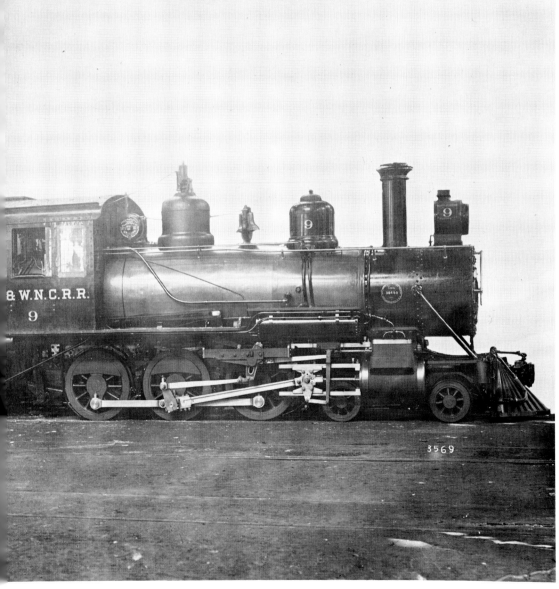

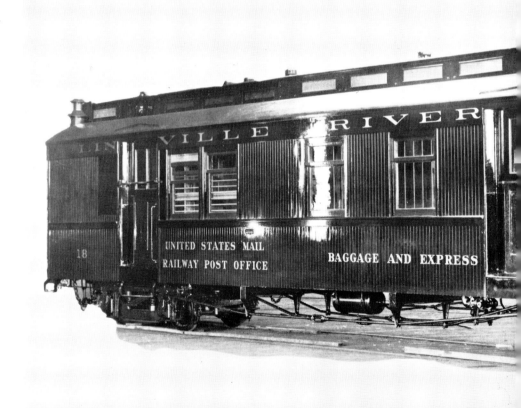

R.P.O. No. 18

Railway Post Office car 18 was built in 1921 by the American Car & Foundry's Jackson & Sharp Works and these rare builder's views show the car when new. — Ed Bond Coll.

E. T. & W. N. C. No. 16

ET&WNC coach 16 was built in 1919 by the Jackson &
Sharp Works. Fine hardwoods were used in her construction. These views were made at the builder's Delaware
plant. — Ed Bond Coll.

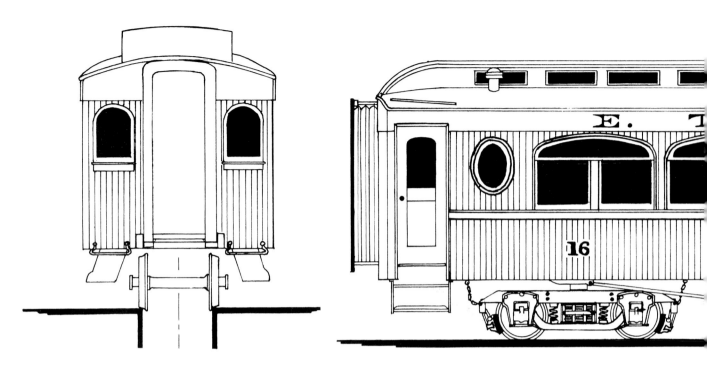

Coach No. 16

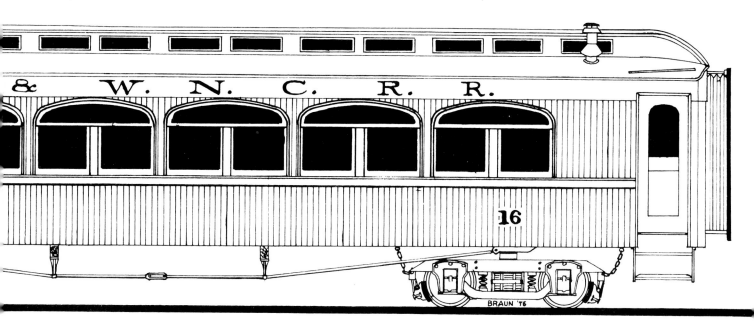

ET&WNC coach 16 is shown in scale drawings by David W. Braun and in detailed photographs at the Jackson & Sharp Works from the collection of Ed Bond. Built in 1919, the car was sold to the Georgia Car & Locomotive Company in 1936 for use on the United Fruit Company's lines.

Coach No. 19

Coach 19 was built by Jackson & Sharp in 1921 and came lettered for the Linville River Railway. Built from the same plans as the ET&WNC 16, the 19 was used in joint LR—ET&WNC passenger service until sold to the United Fruit Company in 1936. These original builder's photographs are from the collection of Ed Bond.

Azalea

Pride of the ET&WNC-LR was Parlor Car 10, the "Azalea," shown on these pages. The "Azalea" trails the daily varnish run at Cranberry (above). — J. T. Dowdy Coll. from Ed Bond. On the opposite page she is shown in the 1920's and on this page lettered for her new owner in Panama in 1936. — Lad Arend from C. W. Hauck.

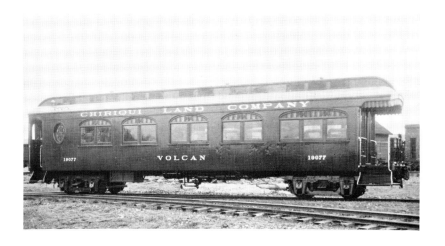

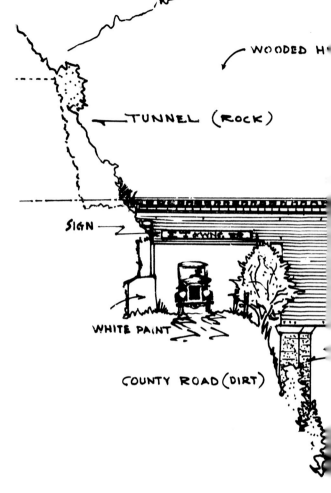

WOODED H

TUNNEL (ROCK)

SIGN

WHITE PAINT

COUNTY ROAD (DIRT)

E. T. & W. N. C.

Covered Bridge,

Covered Bridges

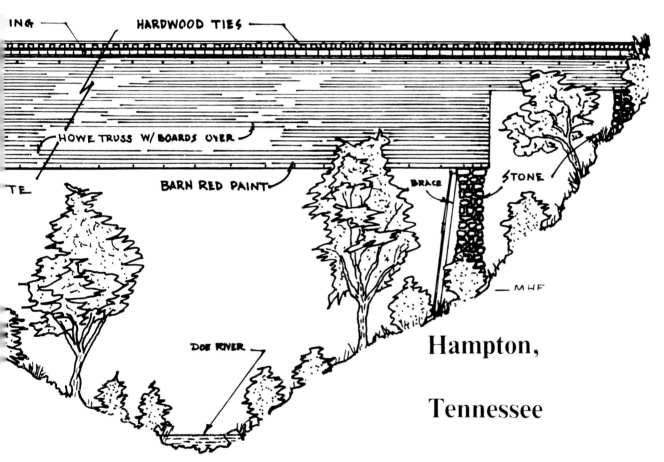

ING

HARDWOOD TIES

HOWE TRUSS W/ BOARDS OVER

TE

BARN RED PAINT

BRACE

STONE

MHF

DOE RIVER

Hampton,

Tennessee

The covered bridges around Hampton were both functional and picturesque. Robert B. Adams was aboard the West-bound freight as it came out of the tunnel and onto the Howe Deck-type bridge (left). The thru-truss bridge East of Hampton is shown (opposite, top) in another Bob Adams view from the 1940's. On this page is a side view of the deck-type bridge over the Doe River, West of Hampton. At the top of this page Cy Crumley stands in front of the Little Doe River bridge East of town.

The Howe through-truss bridge, spanning the Little Doe River is shown on these pages in photographs from Vince Ryan. The pen and ink sketch is by Mike Pearsall.

Locomotive 11 was a favorite with crews on the ET&WNC and she is shown here in two views dating from the mid-1940's. She emerges with a West-bound freight from one of the covered bridges at Hampton (opposite, top) and rounds a curve in the Doe River Gorge. — Lloyd D. Lewis Coll. The rural scene (opposite, lower) taken near Grandfather Mountain, shows a typical Blue Ridge farm in Tweetsie Country.

The Great Depression saw the ET&WNC-LR making-do with very mixed trains and a meager diet of cord wood, l.c.l. freight, mail and what few passengers could be found. Like the people she served, Tweetsie did not have much money. This scene was taken in Linville Gap in 1938 and tells the story. — G. P. Vance.

Please Don't Call Her Tweetsie

The Great Depression did not really come to the remote Blue Ridge hill country in 1929, it was already there. The fortunes of the East Tennessee & Western North Carolina Railroad and the Linville River Railway had begun to slowly decline after World War I and were closely related to those of the parent mining company. The Depression was here in the hills long before they had a fancy $5 bureaucratic name for it.

In 1901, a blast furnace operated by the Virginia Iron, Coal & Coke Company at Johnson City, Tennessee, was leased by the Cranberry Iron & Coal Company. This furnace was purchased outright on February 21, 1905, by the Cranberry Furnace Company, a subsidiary of CI&C. The old hot blast charcoal furnace at Cranberry, North Carolina, built in 1883, was then closed down and ore was separated and concentrated at the original furnace site for shipment to Johnson City. Ore was then hauled over the East Tennessee & Western North Carolina to the blast furnace, which produced about 100 tons of pig iron daily. By 1911, 225 tons of ore was being shipped from the old dumps at Cranberry each day. Additionally, 70 per cent pure magnetite ore was still being mined in three underground stopes, using thirty compressed air drills.

During World War I, mining at Cranberry was expanded and production averaged 60,000 tons annually. The mine was shut down in January, 1921 due to another depression, but opened again in 1923. Operations continued on an ever decreasing basis until 1929, when the mine and the blast furnace closed down.

Even before the stock market crash of "Black Friday" in 1929, the iron ore had been largely depleted, the hillsides had been stripped of most of the timber and the loggers had moved on to greener forests. With the hills stripped of their minerals and timber, the top soil began to wash away. Flooding had always been a problem.

The "May Flood" of 1901 is spoken of by old timers to this very day. It was this flood which had knocked out the private narrow gauge railroad of the Forge Mining Company near Roan Mountain; had taken out all of the bridges in the Doe River Gorge, leaving only the two covered bridges at Hampton. The track was washed out in thirty-nine places and flood damage was so great within the confines of the Gorge that through train service was not resumed until August. In Elizabethton, the only surviving road bridge was the covered bridge across the Doe, that sees service to the present day.

During the rebuilding of the narrow gauge, the general offices were moved from Johnson City to the Cranberry Mine in the summer of 1901. They remained

ET&WNC Number 12 hauls an excursion train between Johnson City and Blevins, Tennessee on July 3, 1938. The Depression-ridden road was beginning to realize the value of special trains and the tourist who rode them. — James P. Shuman.

here until 1903, when they were moved back to Johnson City.

By the early 1930's, the East Tennessee & Western North Carolina and Linville River lines were learning to live with mixed trains and a meager diet of hauling coal, cordwood and whatever general merchandise they could find. The beautiful balsam groves of Grandfather Mountain lived on only in Shepherd Monroe Dugger's little book. The full impact of the Depression had come to the hills.

In 1920, the Linville River part of the line made $150,000 in freight alone. By 1929, with all of the timber cut, the road made $58,000. However, by 1936, revenue on the line dropped to $18,000. With the construction of new paved roads from Johnson City to Boone in 1931, passenger revenue dropped from $11,000 each month to less than $900 and the decline continued with each year.

The East Tennessee & Western North Carolina Railroad's management did not help the narrow gauge and its declining revenues when they formed the ET&WNC Transportation Company to operate passenger busses on December 17, 1926. Later the firm entered the freight trucking business, too. In 1938 the bus line was sold and the freight trucking business expanded. All of this served to cut more deeply into the revenues of the three-foot gauge lines.

In a rare view at Boone, North Carolina, the crew of ET&WNC Number 14 waits for departure time on June 11, 1938. The engine is painted in Clarence Hobbs' "Southern Railway green" with blue (unpainted) Russian Iron boiler jacket and red trim. — Henry E. Bender Collection.

The late Archie Robertson in his *Slow Train To Yesterday* recalls taking a trip aboard the mixed train in 1932 from Linville Gap to Boone. When the conductor came around collecting fares, Archie was a little short. Figuring on his fingers, he said ". . . three and a half cents a mile? Seems a bit steep." The conductor replied "You know, 'hit is too much. I've always thought so. The company sets 'em high on purpose so folks'll ride their busses." The Captain then said "You just give me what you've got there and I'll punch your ticket from Shulls Mills instead."

Despite hard times, the East Tennessee & Western North Carolina and its ward, the Linville River, managed to operate with aging locomotives and cars. Like the people she served, the narrow gauge had little money but a lot of pride.

During the 1930's, Master Mechanic Clarence C. Hobbs created a beautiful paint scheme for the line's locomotives. Everything was painted "Southern Railway green" except the graphite smoke box, running gear and trim. The blue Russian iron boiler jackets were clean, polished and unpainted. Running boards, tires and air compressor heads were silver, while the cap stack, bell and whistle were of polished brass. Cab woodwork was trimmed in red and lettering was in gold.

Engine 14, a beautiful Baldwin 4-6-0 was the first to be repainted, but eventually engines 9, 10, 11, 12 and even the switch engine, Number 7, received the same paint scheme.

In the early days, depots had been painted a dull green with red trim, but during the bleak Depression, the road started painting its buildings in a blue-gray with white trim. Cranberry Iron & Coal Company houses at Johnson City and Cranberry remained in the dull green with red trim colors.

Each day the East Tennessee & Western North Carolina train set forth on her run from Johnson City, past the old house in which President Andrew Johnson had died, by Sycamore Shoals, over the covered bridges of Hampton and through the still beautiful Doe River Gorge, past Crabtree, Roan Mountain, Shell Creek, Elk Park and the likes of Cranberry, Bull Scrape, Love's Crossing, Linville, Jestes Siding, Hodges Gap and Boone. Each year fewer people rode the swaying coaches.

It was Editor Rob Rivers of the *Watauga Democrat* who suggested that the narrow gauge run an excursion train again. These trains had been quite popular until World War I put an end to such pleasuring. The first Sunday excursion in many a year was run in the summer of 1932 from Boone to the Doe River Gorge and back. The excursion trip was so successful that it became a regular attraction on alternate Sundays by the mid-1930's. The excursion trains left Johnson City at 9:00 in the morning and arrived in Boone at 1:30. Returning trains arrived back in Johnson City "about 6:30 p.m." The $1.00 fare covered 130 miles of mountain scenery. Aboard the swaying coaches and chicken wire enclosed excursion cars, the scenic wonders of the Blue Ridge Mountains were available for the looking. A ten minute stop was arranged in the Gorge at Pardee Point. The narrow gauge had rediscovered tourism.

It was during this time that children from the hot lowlands began to come in greater numbers to the many summer camps located near Linville. The 4,000 foot elevations were cool and comfortable and many memories were born during vacations under the shadow of 5,964 foot Grandfather Mountain. Hearing the distant shrill whistle of the daily mixed as it chuffed up the grade, the summer children called the train "Tweetsie."

The hardworking little narrow gauge did not deserve such a sobriquet as "Tweetsie," but the name stuck. In the 1890's, Shepherd Monroe Dugger had noted the train was called "Stemwinder." During the early depression years it was dubbed the "Eat Taters & Wear No Clothes" and "Every Time & With No Complaints" was favored in some quarters. However, it was the misnomer given it by the flatlanders that endured and endeared.

Tweetsie was as full of local color as a railroad could be. Despite a lack of funds and flashy trains, the railroad was a part of the people and the mountains she served. Old timers recall Mrs. Judkins, who lived near Linville Gap and painted beautiful freehand watercolors of Tweetsie as it climbed over a mountain with no sense of gravity, its coach windows filled with waving children.

The mountain people, like the railroad had become self-reliant, many resorting to ancient crafts in order to make their livelihood. Over at Banner Elk, Ed Presnell made the finest dulcimers in the world. Jake Franklin, who lived in the mountains between Pineola and Jonas Ridge was engaged in yet another craft, that of moonshining. Dressed in old clothes, wearing a long beard and carrying a covered basket, he would board the daily mixed train for Johnson City with his family and announce "We'ins goin' to the City." Beneath the checkered cloth cover were a number of bottles of clear corn whiskey. During the Depression years, mountain men had to support themselves and their families and moonshining was considered

86

an honorable trade in the hills by all but the government "Revenooers." Conductor Cy Crumley said that Franklin "made good corn liquor and good apple and peach brandy . . . a little better than Jim Beam."

Here too, the arts of furniture and soap making were still practiced. Five string banjo picking could be heard on a soft summer evening as the mixed train drifted downgrade past a log cabin, the smoke slowly rising from the native stone chimney as the music pierced the cool evening air.

Happy Valley was the home of Bob and Alf Taylor, the fiddling politician brothers. One was a Democrat, the other a Republican and they were often candidates for the same office. One campaigned with a red rose, while the other wore a white rose in his lapel. Their battles were locally referred to as the "War of the Roses."

The East Tennessee & Western North Carolina was known by some folks as the "railroad with a heart." Conductor Cy Crumley obliged with a heart-shaped ticket punch. During the hard times of the 1930's, Cap'n Cy would let needy passengers ride for free saying with a wink "we were going their way anyhow." Quite often Cy would do shopping for the mountain folks at Ed Harbin's General Store in Shulls Mills or at A. P. Brinkley's Clothing & Shoe Store in Elk Park. Cy would take orders one day, do the necessary shopping while the train was switching and deliver the needed goods on the next trip. Cy even delivered a new stove and on one occasion, a coffin! The train would stop anywhere along the line in order to pick up or drop off passengers.

Tweetsie received nationwide attention during the 1930's when Cy Crumley went to far off New York City to appear on the "We The People" radio show. Cy told Gabriel Heatter and Harry von Zell about the time Tweetsie rescued a family from a forest fire, scorching the sides of coach 7 and 2-8-0 Number 4 in the process.

Students at Appalachian State Teachers' College had fun with Tweetsie, too. They would soap the rails on the grade into the Boone yard and then hide behind a tree to watch the ten wheeler spin her 45 inch drivers when Engineer Charlie Miller hit the slippery rails.

In 1939 the East Tennessee & Western North Carolina received more national notoriety when a short feature was filmed about the road. The film was called "Tennessee Tweetsie" and one scene showed Conductor Crumley coaxing a cow from the tracks. Archie Robertson claimed that on an early excursion trip, the train stopped twice for the same cow!

Somehow Tweetsie managed to chuff through the Depression, her diet lean and her revenues little, but with the help of a good crew she made it.

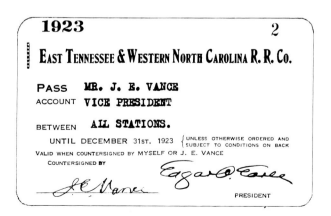

Looka Yonder

Ten-wheeler Number 11 switches a wildflower covered siding (left) in 1938. The cars contain acid wood for a tannery. — G. P. Vance. The daily mixed waits at Boone (above) in 1936. — R. W. Richardson. Artist Mike Pearsall has sketched one of the many signs found on barns throughout Tweetsie Country.

Depression Train

The Depression years were hard times for the Tweetsie and the people she served. The ET&WNC was dubbed the "Eat Taters & Wear No Clothes." The mountain people, like their railroad were upstanding, self-reliant and learned to make-do with what they had. Conductor Cy Crumley would often let hard-pressed families ride for nothing, "we were going their way anyhow" he would say. Above, Number 11 pauses at Linville Gap to let off passengers who lived nearby. The year was 1938 and it was not important that this was not a regular stop. — G. P. Vance. On the opposite page, Mike Pearsall has sketched a family aboard the swaying cars, while the lower view shows bath-day. — Paul A. Moore from Tennessee State Archives.

Johnson City Morning

The main repair shops were at Johnson City. As the sun comes up (above) 4-6-0's pant softly at the enginehouse. — Ed Bond Coll. Number 8 (below) turns on the wye in the early morning of January 24, 1941. — Lawrie Brown Coll. On the opposite page is a view of the shops and Mike Pearsall's sketch of a home-bound engineman.

Mixed Train Daily

Throughout most of her life, Tweetsie had to make-do with a daily mixed train. The combination Railway Post Office-Express-Passenger car provided sufficient accommodations for the few passengers and little head-end traffic. Number 8 is ready to depart from Johnson City (above) on November 30, 1940; while below she treads the dual gauge trackage past the shop area in December of that year. — Lawrie Brown Coll. Artist Mike Pearsall has sketched the interior of one of the ET&WNC-LR depots during this period. "All aboard" for Sycamore Shoals, White Rock, Crab Orchard, Roan Mountain, Shell Creek, Toe Cane and points East!

NOTICE

Mike Pearsall

The ET&WNC needed a full-time switch engine for the growing business in and around Johnson City. In 1906 a powerful little 0-8-0 was ordered from the American Locomotive Company's Brooks Works. When she was delivered in mid-summer, the Number 7 was hailed as the largest narrow gauge engine of her day. She is shown switching the dual gauge trackage (above) in 1930 and (below) at Johnson City in 1940. — Lawrie Brown. On the opposite page, the seven-spot pauses (top), while her builder's photograph is reproduced below.

Johnson City Switcher

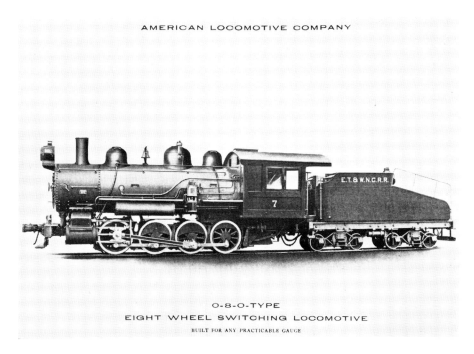

AMERICAN LOCOMOTIVE COMPANY

0-8-0-TYPE
EIGHT WHEEL SWITCHING LOCOMOTIVE
BUILT FOR ANY PRACTICABLE GAUGE

Mike Pearsall

Johnson City Yards

The Johnson City yards were laid with dual-gauge three rail trackage and it was here that all incoming and outgoing loads had to be transferred. Mike Pearsall has drawn a hogger making a switching move (opposite, top). Azaleas are being transferred from narrow gauge cars to one of broad gauge proportions in a R. W. Richardson view taken in 1936 (opposite, lower). On this page, Number 11 is fitted for switching in this 1940 photo. — Lawrie Brown Coll. The dual gauge trackage of the yards is shown below.

The Transfer

Coal and ore was transferred with the unique dual gauge trestle shown here (opposite, top). In these views, coal is being transferred from standard gauge cars into those of the three foot gauge. Wooden hopper car 1 is shown in detail (opposite, lower), while on this page, Robert B. Adams has captured Number 11 at the transfer.

Connections with the World

The ET&WNC connected with the outside world and standard gauge rails at Johnson City and Elizabethton. The "Morning Mail" of the Clinchfield is shown (above) arriving in Johnson City in 1935. Power is CC&O 4-6-0 Number 101. — Steve Patterson Coll. A Southern Ry. connection was made at Johnson City and Elizabethton and typical branch-line power in 1938 was this 4-4-0 Number 3783. — C. W. Witbeck.

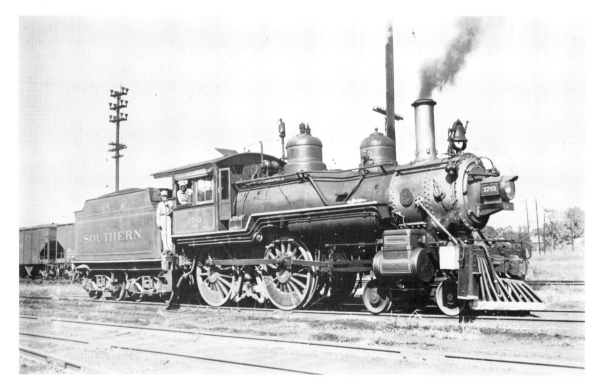

The Clinchfield's 2-8-0 Number 310, shown (above) at Johnson City, may have been bigger than anything on the narrow gauge, but she was not as well maintained. The crew of the standard gauge hog looks from the gangway in Johnson City in 1937. — R. P. Morris. The ET&WNC 12 is shown on dual gauge trackage the same year.

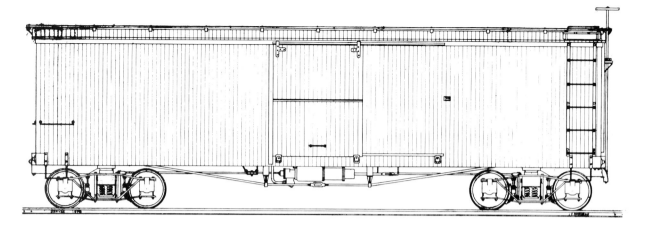

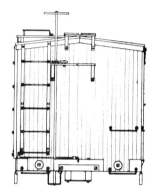

Drawing by John E. Robinson

Scale 3/16″ = 1′-0″

E. T. & W. N. C. — L. R.

Box Car 402

The box cars of the ET&WNC-LR in later years were 36′0″ long, and 7′0″ high. They used a McCord arch-bar truck and were equipped with standard automatic couplers. Cars of both the LR and ET&WNC are shown (below) in a 1942 photo by R. W. Richardson.

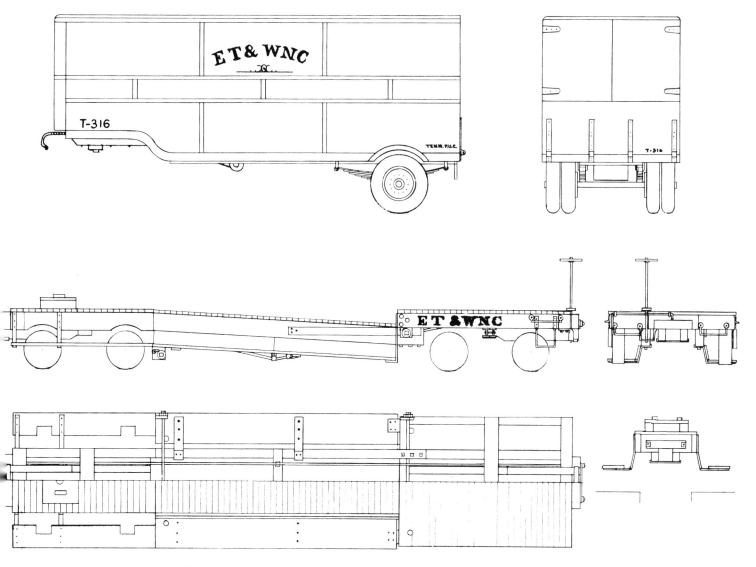

E. T. & W. N. C — L. R. Trailer Car

Shown here is car 800 with Trailer T-316. Cars 565, 801 and 802 were similar. Trucks were same as that used on box car. Colors: box car red frame; trucks-black; lettering-white. Trailer was painted Yellow with brown strip and black lettering. —Ed Bond Coll.

Drawing by John E. Robinson

Scale 3/16″ = 1′-0″

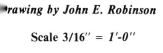

Piggy-Back on the Narrow Gauge

The ET&WNC was one of the first railroads in the United States to use "Piggy-Back" cars. Built in the company shops, these cars carried highway trailers into the remote areas served by the ET&WNC-LR. Car 565 is shown (above) in 1936. One of the unusual cars is included in the consist (below) in the fall of 1936. ET&WNC Number 14 heads out of Johnson City with a mixed train that includes a trailer car and combination baggage-express-RPO-passenger car 15. — R. W. Richardson.

ET&WNC 14 is shown (upper left) in a view from the fireman's seat taken on the Pineola Branch in 1935 by R. W. Richardson. The lower view shows Number 12 with a train of acid wood for the Johnson City tannery, leaving Cranberry on November 18, 1942. — Robert W. Richardson. **On this page, Jack Alexander has captured ET&WNC 11 backing near Hampton in the 1940's.** — Ed Bond Coll.

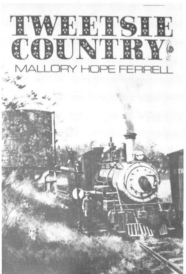

Cranberry, North Carolina saw the daily activity of the ET&WNC and LR and was a favorite spot for photographers and artist of the road. Robert B. Adams captured the view (above) showing Number 11 on the wye with Sherman Pippin at the throttle. Artist Mike Pearsall chose the location for his dust jacket painting for this tome. The 1938 scene (opposite) shows the 11 at Cranberry's water tank. — G. P. Vance Coll.

The ET&WNC and LR used a switchback to get from the Cranberry mainline and upper yards down to the lower yards and depot. Number 11 switches the upper yards (above) in 1941, while Number 12 heads up the switchback in 1942 with a load of acid wood (below and opposite top). — R. W. Richardson. The Number 11 pauses (opposite lower) at the frame depot serving Cranberry in 1941.

Cranberry Switchback

During the depression years, the ET&WNC re-discovered the excursion train. An early outing nears Pardee Point (above) in about 1932. — Ed Bond Coll. The Number 12 leads another excursion near Bemberg Tank in July 1938 (below). — R. W. Richardson. The "Daisy Pickers" are out in force as the Number 10 pauses in the Doe River Gorge in the October 1939 photograph by W. Frank Clodfelter.

Summer's Children

It was the children who came to the summer camps of the Linville Gorge area that gave the ET&WNC a name which lasted . . . "Tweetsie." Campers from Blowing Rock and Banner Elk (above) board the ET&WNC in 1938. Summer's children enjoy Sliding Rock, near Linville (below). — State of North Carolina. The kids mailed home postcards of Tweetsie to parents in the hot cities (opposite top) and rode excursions like that shown behind Number 12 at Newland on the LR in 1938. — R. W. Richardson.

During the summer months before WWII, excursions were a regular event in the Blue Ridge Country. Photographer James P. Shuman has captured just such an outing with Number 12 on July 3, 1938. The train drifts down grade through the Doe River Gorge (above) and climbs Eastbound (opposite top) near Blevins. The excursion is shown (opposite lower) about to depart from Johnson City's depot in the early morning.

Excursion on Tweetsie

While some excursions covered the entire ET&WNC and LR lines, others backed from Johnson City to Blevins and returned home in a normal manner. Number 12 couples an open excursion car to the rear of the train at Blevins on July 3, 1938 in a James P. Shuman photograph. — Broadside from R. W. Richardson Coll.

Last L. R. Excursion

The last excursion over the Linville River Railway was made in October 1938 for the employees of Cannon Mills. The train is shown on these pages near Foscoe with engine 10. The train passed under the shadow of Grandfather Mountain and through Linville Gorge (right). — State of North Carolina.

Daisy-picker's Special

Excursions of the late 1930's used the former BRB&L passenger cars, as the ET&WNC's own cars had been sold for service south of the border. The late Hugh Boutell found Number 12 panting softly as the "Daisy Pickers" took-in the scenery on July 4, 1938 (opposite). On the previous day, James P. Shuman photographed the 12 with cars 22, 23, and 11 in the Doe River Gorge. While on this page, a 1937 excursion is shown near Pardee Point. —Steve Patterson Coll.

Depression Special

A typical consist of the late 1930's was the RPO-Express car and a coach. Train Number 2 is all set to leave Johnson City (above) in 1936. — R. W. Richardson. The 11 leads the same train on June 9, 1939 (right). — Ted Gay from George H. Gregory. Departure time nears (lower right) in a 1935 Johnson City scene.

126

128

Blue Ridge Traveller

To have seen Tweetsie in its narrow gauge glory was to have viewed the most interesting and colorful little mountain railroad in the South. Lucius Beebe phrased it another way, as only he could, after visiting the railroad with his partner Charles Clegg:

"To the reverent pilgrim to have seen Tweetsie is, in a manner of speaking, to have beheld the Veronica, to have bathed in an antiquarian's Ganges. It is the true and absolute of ferrophilia, and we left No. 12 reluctantly to dine off chicken pot pie and Coke at the Coffee Shop in Roan Mountain."

Most of the older passenger equipment had been sold in 1936 to the United Fruit Company for use south of the border. Regular passenger service ended in March 1941, following the flood that knocked out the Linville River Railway, but was reinstated again on August 10, 1942 when the war effort required the daily transportation of many men and women to work in the rayon plant at Bemberg. Three round trips were run each day between Shell Creek and the huge defense plant, the service later being extended to Elk Park in order to bring in workers living in the isolated hill country. Former General Manager George W. Hardin was no longer around to object to Sunday passenger service. Four Laconia Car Company coaches had been obtained secondhand from the Boston, Revere Beach & Lynn, and carried workmen on these wartime trains. The government requisitioned locomotives 10 and 14 for use on the White Pass & Yukon in Alaska.

Following the war, a typical slim gauge freight train left Elizabethton, Tennessee, each morning at ten, daily except Sunday. Pulled by a green, gold and silver ten-wheeler and trailed by a half dozen freight cars, the consist departed the small three-rail yard and headed out over its own three-foot guage rails.

A lunch stop was made at Elk Park and the shade of the depot platform provided a cool place to spend the noon hour, while the crew "shot the bull." Engineer Walter R. Allison would often tell stories to the rest of the crew between bites from a lunchmeat sandwich. Conductor Cy Crumley was seldom without a joke of his own. Fireman C. C. "Brownie" Allison, Walter's nephew, was often the tallpot on this run, with brakemen Mack Luttrell and Clyde Simmerly.

Photographer John Krause has captured Tweetsie in all her glory as Number 11 charges up State Line Hill near Shell Creek in 1950.

Following a brief two mile run to Cranberry, the upper and lower yards were switched before the 4-6-0 was turned on the wye, then the train was again on its way. Some low phosphorous magnetic iron ore was still being mined around Cranberry, but more often the loads consisted of cordwood and coal. Every other Sunday during the summer months an excursion train was run out of Johnson City and the railroad printed up broadsides to announce these trips. When the trains did not run all the way to Cranberry, the engine would "run around" the train and back up on the return trip. Normally these excursions ran as far as Blevins, on the east side of the Doe River Gorge.

The Saturday Evening Post brought attention to the East Tennessee & Western North Carolina in a color story that appeared in April, 1942. With the end of gas and tire rationing after the war, a number of railfan-photographers ventured into the wilds of the hill country to photograph and ride the Tweetsie. Here then is an album of East Tennessee & Western North Carolina photographs by those fortunate enough to have been at trackside with camera in hand; a garland of the Blue Ridge Traveler.

East Tennessee and Western North Carolina Railroad Company
TIME TABLE No. 126
IN EFFECT 12:01 A. M. THURSDAY, MARCH 1, 1945
EASTERN WAR TIME

EASTBOUND				WESTBOUND	
No. 4 Daily P. M.	No. 2 Daily A. M.	Miles	STATIONS	No. 1 Daily A. M.	No. 3 Daily P. M.
		0.	Lve. .... JOHNSON CITY .... Arr.		
		3.6	.... MILLIGAN COLLEGE ....F		
3.15	7.15	7.7	.... PORT RAYON	6.40	2.40
3.21	7.21	9.3	.... ELIZABETHTON (Old Depot) F	6.34	2.34
3.28	7.28	11.2	.... COAL CHUTE ....F	6.27	2.27
3.33	7.33	12.3	.... VALLEY FORGE ....F	6.22	2.22
3.40	7.40	14.1	.... HAMPTON ....F	6.15	2.15
3.59	7.59	19.4	.... BLEVINS ....F	5.56	1.56
4.19	8.19	23.6	.... CRABTREE ....F	5.36	1.36
4.24	8.24	25.6	.... ROAN MOUNTAIN	5.31	1.31
4.30	8.30	27.2	.... SHELL CREEK ....F	5.25	1.25
4.50	8.50	31.9	Arr. ELK PARK Lv.	5.05	1.05
4.50			Lv. ELK PARK Arr.	1.05	
4.55		33.4	Arr. CRANBERRY (Water Tank) Lve.	1.00	
P. M.	A. M.			A. M.	P. M.

F—Flag Stations.

Eastbound trains have right of track over trains of same or lower class in the opposite direction.

No train will follow another closer than FIVE MINUTES.

Inferior trains clear track FIVE minutes before arriving time of Superior trains.

An extra train works daily between Johnson City and East End of yard limits at Elizabethton, with rights over all other extra trains between the hours of 6:00 a. m. and 11:59 p. m.

| C. A. JOHNSON, Trainmaster | CLARENCE HOBBS Superintendent | W. H. BLACKWELL, Vice Pres. and Gen. Mgr. |

130

Passenger service was resumed in August 1942 to help with the war effort. The timetable shows the four daily trains operated to Elk Park. — R. W. Richardson Coll. **Photographer Hugh Morton found ET&WNC Number 11 with a post-war freight blasting through Elk Park in January 1946.**

Train's A comin'

Ten wheeler Number 11 picks up speed as she leaves Johnson City on three rail trackage (above) with engineer Sherman Pippin at the throttle. It is the summer of 1941. The same train blasts up the three percent grade of the Doe River Gorge (opposite) at Pardee Point. — Both photos by Robert B. Adams. **Engineer Pippin pauses in the Gorge (below), in a 1938 excursion scene.** — Hugh Boutell

Water Stop

The water tank at Bemberg, Tennessee was a normal stop for all trains. The 11 leaves the tank (above) on August 5, 1941 after taking water (opposite) at the tank. — Robert B. Adams

134

Clegg on Tweetsie

Photographer Charles Clegg visited the ET&WNC in January 1946, while he and Lucius Beebe were preparing *Mixed Train Daily*, the book that started a railfan movement. Here Clegg has photographed ten wheeler Number 12 as she heads East out of Hampton, Tennessee and over the Howe Truss Covered Bridge spanning the Little Doe River. On the opposite page, artist Casey Holtzinger has drawn the 11 as she storms out of the same structure.

Doe River Gorge

The twisting trackage of the Doe River Gorge contained four tunnels. On this page, photographer Robert B. Adams has captured the Number 11 as she eases across a bridge and into tunnel Four on August 5, 1941 with a west bound freight. On the opposite page, the 11 works upgrade out of Tunnel Four. — Robert B. Adams. The small view shows the Gorge trackage as the train exits a tunnel, crosses a bridge and goes into another tunnel. — Lloyd Lewis Coll.

In the Gorge

The remote setting of the Doe River Gorge provides the background for those Robert B. Adams photographs showing a west bound freight extra headed by 4-6-0 Number 11. The date is August 5, 1941. The 11 eases downgrade out of Tunnel Four onto a Deck Truss bridge in a fine set of action photographs. The small view shows the entrance to a rock tunnel. — Lloyd Lewis Coll.

140

Tennessee Gothic

Lucius Beebe found ET&WNC 12 working upgrade in 1946 in the fine view at left. Beebe and his partner, Charles Clegg then dined at S. B. Wood's establishment in Roan Mountain, Tennessee and made the place famous when they wrote about it in *Mixed Train Daily*. The daily freight is shown (below) at the Roan Mountain depot in the summer of 1941, headed by the Number 11, in a scene from the Tennessee gothic setting of the small town.

Noon Time Stop at Elk Park

It is lunch time on the ET&WNC and the crew has paused at the Elk Park depot to eat and exchange jokes in the shade of the platform and nearby overhanging trees. — Robert B. Adams. **In a rare view showing two trains out on the line, a wartime freight eases past a passenger train at Elk Park on October 19, 1944.** — William S. Cannon

ET&WNC 12 raises a plume of smoke and her safety valve pops off beside the Cranberry, North Carolina depot in June 1946. The fine view was taken by Charles M. Clegg. On the opposite page, R. W. Richardson found the 12 at the Cranberry water tank in 1942 and Jack Alexander photographed the Number 11 while she switched the yards behind the general store. — Ed Bond Coll.

The wartime passenger trains of the ET&WNC are shown on these pages, as a train headed by Number 11 turns on the Bemberg wye (above and lower right) and prepares to leave the Elizabethton depot (upper right). — Pete Cornwall Col. The Number 9 meets the 11 at Port Rayon (below) on November 18, 1942 in a R. W. Richardson photograph.

ET&WNC 12 arrives in Elk Park (above) during 1942 with a short east bound train. — R. W. Richardson. The tender view was made by the late Jack Alexander near Elizabethton. Caboose 505 was built in the company shops and was photographed by R. W. Richardson in 1942.

War Time Freight

It is early morning and Number 9 (above) is all set to depart from Elk Park with a war time commuter train. Later in the day, ET&WNC 11 would bring the same cars back to Elk Park (top opposite), where she met Number 12 which had arrived with a freight train (lower views). The photographs were made on November 18, 1942 by R. W. Richardson.

Old No. 8 Finds Another Job

When the ET&WNC sold their first Number 8 in 1920, the ten wheeler finished out her days hauling logs for the Gray Lumber Company at Waverly, in eastern Virginia. On these pages the late Reverend William Gwaltney has pictured the 4-6-0 in service on the log road in 1950. The side view (opposite lower) was made by H. Reid in 1948.

ET&WNC freight, June 1946. — By Charles M. Clegg

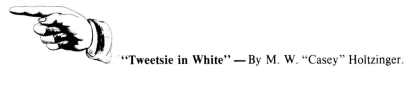 **"Tweetsie in White"** — By M. W. "Casey" Holtzinger.

Tweetsie Calls it Quits

Due to declining revenues, especially on the Linville River Railway portion of the narrow guage, maintenance was "cut to the bone" and bridges, culverts and fills were allowed to become weed-grown. General Manager W. H. Blackwell said "We didn't spend a dime we didn't have to." The Tennessee Valley Authority (TVA) had not yet made enough progress deep in the hills to control flooding.

The hills themselves had been stripped of their minerals and timber. Following several days of heavy, steady rain, a severe flood washed out major parts of the Linville River line on August 13, 1940, shortly after the daily mixed train had arrived in Cranberry on its run to Johnson City. Many portions of the track were gone, bridges and fills were washed away, while heavy mud slides covered much of the remaining rails. Equipment at Boone and other points along the line was isolated and stranded.

President A. G. B. Steele came down from Philadelphia to inspect the damage and was not of a mind to rebuild the Linville River Railway. After a Sunday meeting with Dr. B. B. Dougherty of the Appalachian State Teachers' College, Mayor W. R. Lovill and others in Boone, W. H. Blackwell offered to sell the washed-out railroad to the township for one dollar. However, when Dr. Dougherty wrote up the proposition, the company declined the offer. The truth of the matter is that the railroad had applied to abandon the entire line the day before the Boone meeting took place on September 5, 1940.

The cost of repairing the Linville River Railway was estimated at $158,838, while the salvage value was set at $53,450 for the 31.57 miles of line. During the preceeding three years the line had lost almost ten thousand dollars and for the first eight months of 1940 had shown a profit of only $668.

The Linville River applied to abandon its tracks on September 4, 1940. A hearing was set for 10:00 a.m. at the John Sevier Hotel in Johnson City on November 29, 1940. Interstate Commerce Commission Examiner Schutrumpf heard the case which was highlighted by testimony from Dr. Dougherty on behalf of keeping the narrow gauge. The professor told of the efforts to get the tracks extended into Boone and how the town had paid the railroad $20,000 in bonds over the years and was still willing to pay the remaining $7,000 if the railroad could be put

The last train of them all on the East Tennessee & Western North Carolina, as photographed by John Krause on October 16, 1950.

back in operation. General Superintendent W. H. Blackwell then took the stand to describe the line. He said "It just follows the general contour, up hill and down hill and around curves and across creeks and rivers." Examiner Schutrumpf asked: "Just like a bull calf would go?" Blackwell answered: "In some places I doubt if a bull calf could get there."

In the hill country, it is customary to say a few words when a close friend passes away. Young Annette Vance of Minneapolis, North Carolina (pop. 53), wrote to Examiner Schutrumpf asking him to save the train. Her poem was entitled "A Hill Billie's Lament."

In Carolina how it did rain,
It took from us a little train.
So long it seems since we heard her blow,
I wonder why it could thus be so.
Our Tweetsie who we loved so dear,
Her coming and going we have ceased to hear,
Our little train we loved so well.
And our love for her in our hearts doth dwell.
Dear God, is this hope in vain?
Send us back our little train.
The waters rose and took her track,
We want our little Tweetsie back.
What could we do or what could we say,
To get her back the same old way?
Now we can't even hear a train blow.
Are we civilized, oh who can know,
When she passed, we stood amazed,
We admired her so, we stood and gazed.
Her loss we pine, we loved her so.
To think we will never hear her blow.
Our memory of her is clear and plain.
Please send us back our little train.

The high price of scrap and the hard cold facts of railroad finance won out and the Linville River Railway was allowed to abandon its line on March 22, 1941. Equipment on the isolated portion of the line was trucked out to be used on the remaining East Tennessee & Western North Carolina trackage. The rails of the Linville River line were sold to Midwest Steel Company of Charleston, West Virginia.

The same flood that knocked out the Linville River Railway also washed out much of the Southern Railway's Virginia & Southern Railway line between Elizabethton and Mountain City, Tennessee. Standard gauge cars from this line were hauled over the highway to Hampton and then taken out over the third rail of Tweetsie's line. The outside rail was then removed from a point just east of the Elizabethton coal chute (O'Brien) to Hampton.

With the abandonment of the Linville River, the East Tennessee & Western North Carolina continued to operate on dual gauge trackage from Johnson City to Elizabethton and as a three-foot gauge line from Elizabethton to Cranberry. A standard gauge 2-8-0 had been purchased secondhand in 1927 to switch the dual gauge trackage, but mainline passenger and freight runs had continued to be hauled by narrow gauge engines.

Tweetsie, as a narrow gauge railroad, continued to run until the autmn of

1950. Revenues on the remaining narrow gauge continued to decline and passenger service was dropped again following the War. Most trains on the three-foot gauge tied up at Elizabethton, as standard gauge engines were now handling most of the traffic on the dual gauge lines. Following approval of an abandonment request on the trackage from O'Brien to Cranberry, the company officials made a farewell trip over the line on September 24, 1950. The Sunday special was hauled by Number 11 and included combine 15 and open excursion car 11 on a Cranberry round trip. This was the last passenger train over the line.

The last regular freight train run was made on October 16, 1950. It was a bright, clear, warm day when 4-6-0 Number 11 left Elizabethton at 10:10 a.m. with seven cars. In the cab were Walter Allison and "Brownie" Allison. Back in the caboose, where he had served for more than 44 years, was Cy Crumley with brakemen Clyde Simmerly and Mack Luttrell.

The train arrived in Elk Park at 12:15 after a run up State Line Hill. The crew retired to the depot platform as they had done for so many years. However, the normal conversation was absent today, as the railroaders looked back on a career on the narrow gauge. Nostalgia seemed to take hold this day and the usual lunchtime jokes were noticeably missing. The men could only think that this was the last run and no longer would they sit here in the shade, watching the now aging ten-wheeler pant softly beneath the giant shade trees.

After some brief switching, the train continued the few remaining miles to Cranberry. Here two gondolas loaded with track tools were left for the scrappers and Number 11 was spotted beneath the water tank for the final time. On the return trip, folks came out from small cabins to wave goodbye to an old friend as she passed Shell Creek and Roan Mountain.

Extra 11 west ended regular narrow gauge operations when she pulled into the Elizabethton yards at 3:30 p.m. The Tweetsie that everyone loved was gone.

ET&WNC 11 leads an east bound freight in the final year of operation. — Photograph by Harold K. Vollrath.

Post War Freight

Photographer Ray Tobey found ET&WNC 12 and a freight near Elk Park (opposite top) and steaming along near Hampton (above) in April 1948. At lower left is a view of State Line Hill, just west of Elk Park. — Robert B. Adams.

163

End of the L. R. Ry.

A flood that struck Tweetsie Country on August 13, 1940 spelled the end of the Linville River Railway. The tracks between Cranberry and Boone were washed-out, bridges and fills were washed away and heavy mud covered the remaining rails. Across the top of these two pages are three pictures of the scrap train that removed the LR rails. — Ed Bond Coll. **Remaining cars had to be hauled out over the road (below).** — J. T. Dowdy. Pen and ink sketch by Mike Pearsall.

164

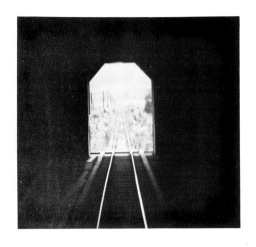

Tweetsie's Last Run

The last run on the ET&WNC narrow gauge occurred October 16, 1950. Here we see 4-6-0 Number 11 west bound at Hampton, Tennessee, as she takes the last train across the covered bridge toward Elizabethton. Covered bridges had been a part of the daily life in Tweetsie Country since the 1880's. Above are two views of the bridge at Hampton, while below is the bridge across the Doe River at Elizabethton, still in use today. — Photographs by John Krause (opposite), Robert B. Adams (upper left) and Lloyd Lewis (upper right).

166

Bifocal Line

Despite broad gauge aspirations of the 1860's, the East Tennessee & Western North Carolina Railroad was constructed as a narrow gauge road in the 1880's. All incoming and outgoing shipments had to be reloaded at Johnson City or Elizabethton, a time consuming and expensive transfer.

The narrow gauge connected with the Southern Railway and Carolina, Clinchfield & Ohio Railway at Johnson City; while connections were made with the Laurel Fork Railway and the Virginia & Southern Railway at Eliazbethton. All of these roads operated on standard 4-foot, 8½-inch gauge trackage.

When the changeover from link and pin to automatic couplers was made in 1903-04, coupler height of the narrow gauge equipment was raised to that of the standard gauge. A unique swivel arrangement on the locomotives allowed narrow gauge engines to couple with standard gauge cars in the dual gauge yard at Johnson City.

On June 15, 1903, the conversion of 9.5 miles of mainline between Johnson City and Elizabethton was authorized. A third rail was laid on longer ties between May 1904 and December 1906. In 1907, the Furnace Spur was jointly built with the Southern Railway. This 1.482 mile branch served the Cranberry Furnace Company's blast furnace at Carnegie. Another three rail line was constructed in 1910 between Buffalo Bridge (Watauga Point) and Smallings, Tennessee. This line was known as the Watauga River Spur and it served a large gravel and sand pit.

In April, 1910, A. Rex Flynn, owner of the Pittsburg Lumber Company, chartered the Laurel Fork Railway Company to build a line from Hampton, on the East Tennessee & Western North Carolina, to the Frog Level area, about five miles. Flynn's firm owned the timber on 6,000 acres north of Hampton.

Mr. Flynn and George W. Hardin, General Manager of the East Tennessee & Western North Carolina had a dispute over freight rates for Pittsburg Lumber Company timber between Hampton and Elizabethton, so on December 8, 1910 the *Manufacturers Record* reported that construction of a standard gauge railroad from Elizabethton "had begun to Hampton, Boone and Wilkesboro, North Carolina." Hardin and Flynn were at such odds that Flynn decided to give Tweetsie some competition. By June, 1911, the seven miles of trackage between Elizabethton and

ET&WNC standard gauge 2-8-0 Number 208 switches the Textile mill at Bemberg, Tennessee on April 28, 1966.

169

Hampton had been completed by Flynn's crews. An additional 11 miles were planned to connect the mill at Braemar with the timber on Pond Mountain, around Frog Level and Laban, Tennessee.

By 1913, the Laurel Fork Railway was in operation for 17 miles between Elizabetthton, Braemar, Crows, Frog Level asd Laban. The line was operated as a logging railroad for freight service only. A. Rex Flynn must have given up on his idea of putting the East Tennessee & Western North Carolina out of business. The Laurel Fork Railway operated on the opposite side of the Doe River and used several Shay locomotives and 30 logging cars. The hardwood band mill at Braemar was among the largest in the Appalachians and the logging tracks out of the mill town used an 8 per cent grade.

The dispute between Pittsburg Lumber Company and the East Tennessee & Western North Carolina cost the railroad an estimated $85,000 in revenues each year. The Laurel Fork began pulling back its logging tracks in 1925 and by 1927 the line had been abandoned and most of the rails removed.

The East Tennessee & Western North Carolina Railroad extended its third rail from Elizabethton to Hampton in 1911 so they could bring out finished lumber from the W.M. Ritter mill located there. This standard gauge rail was removed in 1941.

In 1927 the East Tennessee & Western North Carolina purchased their first standard gauge locomotive, a second-hand Consolidation from the Norfolk & Western. Narrow gauge locomotives continued to power regular freight and passenger runs, while the standard gauge engine switched around Johnson City and Elizabethton.

As the East Tennessee countryside between the two towns became more industrialized, standard gauge engines took over a greater share of the switching and road work between Johnson City and Elizabethton. Following the abandonment of the three-foot gauge trackage in 1950 and the removal of the narrow gauge rail, the road used a number of second-hand locomotives on the 11 miles of remaining trackage.

ET&WNC 208 heads east bound out of Johnson City over what was once broad gauge, then narrow gauge, three rail dual gauge and finally standard gauge trackage.

Pride of the line in later years was a pair of former Southern Railway 2-8-0s that were obtained in 1952. The two Consolidations were kept in beautiful condition at the Johnson City Legion Street enginehouse. Superintendent Clarence Hobbs had the engines painted in the green, gold and silver of narrow gauge days and shopman D. A. Palmer and J. Andrew Kerns saw to it that the engines were wiped down and kept shining. With no turning facilities, the engines always faced westward.

Alternating in service, the 207 and 208 often had to double the hill on the 2.4 per cent grade up Milligan Hill. Cy Crumley was still serving as conductor and C. C. "Brownie" Allison was engineer, with Earl Vest holding down the left cab seat. Brakemen Dee Whitson, Earl McKinney and extra brakeman-inspector, Jim Dowdy completed the train crew. Trainmaster L. H. Harrell, two shopmen, three agents and an eight-man section crew completed the payroll.

The two Consolidations were so rare that fans came from all over the country to see, photograph and record their wanderings. During the fall of 1960, the Number 207 pulled an excursion from Johnson City to Kingsport, Tennessee, over the Clinchfield as part of the National Railway Historical Society's National Convention that was held in Bristol. In 1962, engine 208 went to Knoxville, Tennessee, to play a part in the Hollywood production of "All The Way Home."

The Southern Railway was searching for suitable engines for their steam excursion and public relations runs, started by the system's railfan-Vice President-Law (now President) W. Graham Claytor, Jr. They offered to trade a pair of Diesels for the two steamers.

Friday, December 8, 1967 was the final day of steam operation on the East Tennessee & Western North Carolina. The 207 was repainted and overhauled as Southern Number 630, while sister 208 was relettered to her former Southern Number 722. The two joined another famous green and gold Southern locomotive, 2-8-2 Number 4501, in excursion service throughout the South.

Consolidation 208 passes the old narrow gauge enginehouse at Elizabethton on April 28, 1966. The end of track lies just to the east at the coal chute.

Bemberg Water Stop

Bemberg Tank, which once served the narrow gauge trains of the ET&WNC provided water for the standard gauge engines as well. On this page, Number 208 eases into position under the spout (above), while the 207 takes water (opposite top). Fireman Earl Vest is shown at the same tank. — Steve Patterson.

Meet at Bemberg

The North American Rayon Corporation operates its own plant switcher at Bemberg. The fireless "cooker", Number 1, meets ET&WNC Number 207 (above) in 1967. — Lloyd Lewis. The fireless 0-6-0 was built by Porter (below). — Steve Patterson. On the opposite page, Fireman Earl Vest looks from the cab of 2-8-0 Number 208. Even in standard gauge days, the ET&WNC kept their engines in fine shape.

The ET&WNC kept their former Southern Railway 2-8-0's in good repair and track maintenance was also good. Drawing by Mike Pearsall. The 208 is shown (above) at Elizabethton, while the 207 is depicted at speed (below) in a Steve Patterson photograph.

A Pair of Rare 2-8-0's

In 1962, ET&WNC 208 traveled to Knoxville, Tennessee to take part in the filming of "All The Way Home." — Thomas Lawson, Jr. Sister 207 hauled an excursion over Clinchfield rails for the National Railway Historical Society in 1960 (below) — Steve Patterson. In 1967 the Southern Railway traded the ET&WNC a pair of diesels for the 2-8-0's. Southern renumbered the ex-ET&WNC engines to their original SR numbers and put them in excursion use. The 630 is shown at Columbia, S.C. in 1970 (opposite left) and the 722 is shown near Vaucluse, S. C. — Al Langley and Mary Langley photos. The 208 is shown (opposite) at Bemberg in 1966, while the 207 is pictured as SR 630 at Irondale, Ala, in a pair of photos by Thomas Lawson, Jr.

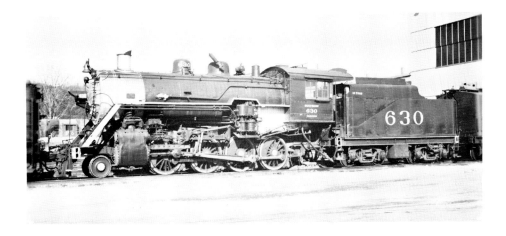

Tweetsie Comes Home

There is a saying among the Blue Ridge mountain people that goes: "You can take the boy out of the hills, but you can never take the hills out of the boy." The memory of sitting on the end of a narrow gauge crosstie, amid the heat of a July afternoon, eating a peanut butter and jelly sandwich while listening for the distant sounds of the steam train as she snaked her way through the Doe River Gorge, is now a fond memory of youth.

More than twenty years have passed since the narrow gauge trains themselves left those hills. The tracks have long been torn-up and their path is kept fresh only by the occasional wanderings of a dairy cow or spring fisherman. But, in many a smoky hollow, old timers recall stories of Tweetsie. The railroad was itself a part of the hills and the hill people she served, and when the narrow gauge was torn-up, it was like a part of them had died.

In 1952, locomotive Number 12 and two cars were purchased by three dedicated railfans from Harrisonburg, Virginia, after ET&WNC President Alfred Steel lowered the price of the equipment so that it could be saved. The equipment was moved to a farm six miles east of Harrisonburg, at Penn Laird. It was here that C. Gratten Price, Jr., Doctor Paul S. Hill and Wade W. Menefee, Jr. built a one mile loop of trackage for the Shenandoah Central Railroad. Number 12 was steamed-up and put in service on the new line for the first time on Memorial Day of 1953, pulling a consist of former Combination-Railway Post Office car Number 15; ex-ET&WNC Excursion car 11 and a former East Broad Top coach.

The former ET&WNC equipment was restored to its orginial paint scheme and operated on weekends from May through early October. Then disaster struck on October 15, 1953 in the form of Hurricane Hazel, which washed away most of the trackage and in general laid waste to the entire Shenandoah Valley. For a brief time, cowboy motion picture star Gene Autry held an option on the equipment of the Shenandoah Central Railroad. Autry planned to move the cars and 4-6-0 to his California "Melody Ranch." However in 1955, Grover C. Robbins, Jr. of Lenoir, North Carolina purchased the locomotive and three cars and brought them home to the hills. On a mountain near Blowing Rock, Robbins set about building his reincarnated Tweetsie Railroad. The equipment was shipped south to Hickory,

Tweetsie came home to the Blue Ridge hills aboard a standard gauge flat car. Here a crowd welcomes ET&WNC Number 12 on May 24, 1956 at Hickory, North Carolina. — North Carolina State Photograph by Bill Gulley.

North Carolina in early May of 1956. May 20th was declared "Tweetsie Home Coming Day" by Governor Luther Hodges, and a big celebration was held on May 24th when "Tweetsie" arrived aboard a standard gauge flatcar. Following a rebuilding in the Carolina & Northwestern shops, the equipment was loaded aboard five flat-bed trailers for the move from Hickory to Blowing Rock on May 23, 1957. She was placed on a section of track at the newly renamed Roundhouse Mountain site on Highway 221-321 between Boone and Blowing Rock and steamed-up again. With a full head of steam, the Number 12 went into service on the 4th of July, 1957. Engineer Frank Coffey ran the short train over the 225 foot long, 50 foot high trestle to the end of the track, a mile away, then backed the consist down to the depot. Within a short time the trackage formed a complete circle around the mountain.

The plea of a little girl from the Blue Ridge Mountains to the all-powerful Interstate Commerce Commission to "Please send us back our little train" had been at last answered. Tweetsie was home again.

Following the abandonment of the narrow gauge, ET&WNC 12 and two cars went to a Virginia farm, where they operated on the privately owned Shenandoah Central Railroad, at Penn Laird. — Drawing by Mike Pearsall.

Shenandoah Central

The Shenandoah Central Railroad operated on a one mile loop near Harrisonburg, Virginia. Former ET&WNC 12 is shown in the summer of 1953. Hurricane Hazel destroyed the line in October of that year. — Opposite lower view by August Thieme from Henry E. Bender Coll.

Tweetsie Railroad

In 1955, the late Grover Robbins purchased the equipment of the Shenandoah Central and moved it to a mountain location near Blowing Rock, North Carolina in the heart of Tweetsie Country. It was here that Robbins set about building his reincarnated Tweetsie Railroad. The former ET&WNC 4-6-0 and cars went into service on July 4, 1957, complete with phoney hold-ups.

E. T. & W. N.

DATE JUN

TRAIN	ENGINEER	FIREMAN	CONDUCTOR	B'...
6	PIPPIN	VEST	D. Simerly	Co... Flet...
10	W.R. Allison	F. Allison	Sisk	Ble... Lu...
2	J. Miller	C. Simerly	Ferrell	Ho... Bo...
Ex 14	Ford	Lacy	C. Angel	Gre... MP...
8	WILL NOT RUN Today			Cr...
12	C. Miller	P. Fletcher	Jobe	Her... B. Si...

Mike Pearsall

10

Tweetsie Roster

The orginal East Tenness & Western North Carolina broad gauge line of 1866 never owned any equipment of its own and in fact, never got into operation. The only train movements over the five foot gauge line were powered by a 4-4-0 of the East Tennessee, Virginia & Georgia Railroad (Southern) in 1872. With the 1875 reorganization and the decision to rebuild the line of three-foot gauge, came the first equipment owned and operated by the road. The first locomotive arrived in 1880 and was a Baldwin mogul. Another 2-6-0 followed in 1881, and then came four consolidations over the next twenty-two years. A lone Brooks 0-8-0 in 1906 was followed by the "standard power" of the road, a fleet of Baldwin ten wheelers delivered between 1907 and 1919. The first standard gauge engine, a former Norfolk & Western 2-8-0, came to the ET&WNC in 1927.

East Tennessee & Western North Carolina 10 poses at Johnson City in 1938 in a classic engine view by John B. Allen. Mike Pearsall has sketched the train order board as it was on a summer day in 1929.

NARROW GAUGE
LOCOMOTIVES OF THE EAST TENNESSEE & WESTERN NORTH CAROLINA
AND LINVILLE RIVER RAILROADS

NO.	TYPE	BUILDER	CONST. NO.	DATE	CYLINDERS	DRIVERS	REMARKS
1	2-6-0	Baldwin	5403	12/1880	14 × 18	39	"Watauga" Sold Newell & Bryant Lbr. Co. 1912, Stoney Creek, Virginia.
2	2-6-0	Baldwin	5746	8/1881	14 × 18	39	"Cranberry" Sold Hilton Lbr. Co. #14, 1910 Wilmington, N.C.
3	2-8-0	Baldwin	6377	9/1882	15 × 18	36	"Unaka" Sold to Fosburgh Lbr. Co. #8, 1911 Fosburgh, N.C.
4	2-8-0	Baldwin	21114	10/1902	15 × 20	37	Scrapped 1940's.
5	2-8-0	Baldwin	21893	3/1903	15 × 20	37	To Linville River #5, scrapped.
6	2-8-0	Baldwin	24734	9/1904	15 × 20	37	Scrapped 1930's.
7	0-8-0	Brooks	39951	6/1906	17 × 20	44	Scrapped c. 1940.
8	4-6-0	Baldwin	31479	8/1907	15 × 20	45	To Gray Lbr. Co. #8, c. 1920 Waverly, Va. Scrapped.
2nd 8	4-6-0	Baldwin	37327	12/1911	15 × 22	45	Original Twin Mountain & Potomac R.R. #2, To Rapidan R.R. #2, Orange, Va. 4/1921, To ET&WNC 2nd 8 10/26/1926. Scrapped.
9	4-6-0	Baldwin	36440	4/1911	15 × 22	45	To Linville River #9, ET&WNC #9. Scrapped.
10	4-6-0	Baldwin	42766	1/1916	16 × 22	45	To U.S. Government for White Pass & Yukon #10, 1942 Skagway, Alaska. Damaged in roundhouse fire at Whitehorse 12/1943, returned to Seattle and scrapped 12/1945.
11	4-6-0	Baldwin	42862	6/1916	16 × 22	45	Scrapped 1952.
12	4-6-0	Baldwin	45069	2/1917	16 × 22	45	To Shenandoah Central Railroad, Harrisonburg, Va. 1952. To Tweetsie Railroad, Blowing Rock, N.C. 1955. In service.
14	4-6-0	Baldwin	52406	9/1919	16 × 22	45	To U.S. Government for White Pass & Yukon #14, 1942, Skagway, Alaska. Damaged in roundhouse fire at Whitehorse 12/1943, returned to Seattle and scrapped 12/1945.
28	2-6-0	Baldwin	39697	8/1913	15 × 22	38	Original Kentwood & Eastern #28, to Linville River #28, 1918. Scrapped.

190

ET&WNC 4 waits out the years at Johnson City in 1938. — R. W. Richardson. **The Number 5 (center) was a Linville River engine.** — Lawrie Brown Coll. **Switcher 7 was largest narrow gauge engine when built in 1906. She is shown at Johnson City in 1938.** — Hugh G. Boutell.

After 1907, all new locomotives ordered by the ET&WNC were Baldwin 4-6-0's. Second Number 8 (top) came second hand in 1926, but was like the 9 (center). Both were built in 1911. — Lawrie Brown Coll. and C. W. Witbeck. The 10 came new in 1916 and went to the White Pass & Yukon during WWII. — Ted Gay from George Gregory Coll.

ET&WNC ten wheeler 11 saw a great deal of service during the last years of the line. She is shown (top) in 1950. — John Krause. The Number 12 (center) is the last ET&WNC narrow gauge engine in existence. She is shown at Johnson City in 1948. — Harold K. Vollrath. Number 14 went to the WP&Y in 1942, and is shown at Johnson City in 1940 (lower) in a photo by Robert N. Hanft. — Henry E. Bender Coll.

Linville River Railway 28 was built for the Kentwood & Eastern in Louisiana and came to the LR in 1918. The 28 is shown at Johnson City in 1925. In the lower view, the 28 is shown on the dead line in 1936. — Tom Lawson, Jr. Coll.

In the June 1941 view (above) ET&WNC power from the left is 14, 11, 12, 204 and 205. —
Jim Bower Coll. In 1926 Baldwin designed a Mallet 2-6-6-2 for the ET&WNC, based on the
engines built for the Uintah Railway in far off Colorado. The Great Depression spelled an
end to dreams of articulated power on the ET&WNC-LR. — Ed Bond Coll.

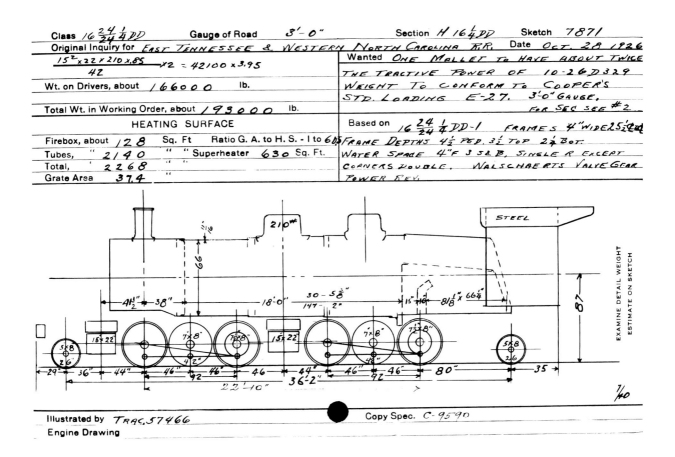

Illustrated by *TRAC. 57466*

Engine Drawing

Copy Spec. *C-9590*

STANDARD GAUGE
LOCOMOTIVES OF THE EAST TENNESSEE & WESTERN NORTH CAROLINA RAILROAD
(ET&WNC ceased operations August 1, 1983, reorganized as East Tennessee Railway)

NO.	TYPE	BUILDER	CONST. NO.	DATE	CYLINDERS	DRIVERS	REMARKS
828	2-8-0	Baldwin	16858	7/1899	21 × 30	56	Formerly Norfolk & Western #828, to ET&WNC #828, 1927. First standard gauge locomotive. Scrapped 8/1937.
204	2-8-0	Lima	6239	2/1922	20 × 24	46	Original Alabama, Tennessee & Northern #204. Scrapped c. 1955.
205	0-6-0	Baldwin	29768	12/1906	20 × 26	50	Formerly Richmond, Fredricksburg & Potomac 104, 13. Sold to Cadiz R.R. #205 c. 1953, to Crabtree Coal Co. #205, St. Charles, Ky.
206	2-6-0	Brooks	3693	12/1900	20 × 28	63	Formerly Illinois Central #556. Retired 1955 and scrapped, 1956.
207	2-8-0	Richmond	28446	2/1904	24 × 30	56	Formerly Southern Ry. #630, purchased 12/1952. Traded 1967 to Southern Ry. and renumbered #630.
208	2-8-0	Baldwin	24729	9/1904	24 × 30	56	Formerly Southern Ry. #722, purchased 11/1952. Traded 1967 to Sou. Ry. #722. Excursion use.

NO.	DIESEL	BUILDER	CONST. NO.	DATE	REMARKS
209	RS-3	Alco-GE	78246	9/1950	Formerly Central of Georgia #108. From Southern Ry. 1967. To Elizabethton Herb & Metal 10/1987 and scrapped.
210	RS-3	Alco-GE	78247	9/1950	Formerly Central of Georgia #109. From Southern Ry. 1967. To Elizabethton Herb & Metal 10/1987; to Roanoke Valley Central RR (restoration group) 1990. Restored as C. of Ga. 109.
211	RS-32	Alco-GE	84027	3/1962	Formerly Southern Pacific 7302, 4002; ET&WNC 211, East Tennessee 211.
212	RS-32	Alco-GE	83981	6/1961	Formerly NYC 8020, Penn Central 2035, Conrail 2035; Md. & Del. 40; ET&WNC 212, E.T. 212.

Standard gauge motive power of the ET&WNC started with a former N&W 2-8-0 (top) acquired in 1927 and pictured at Johnson City in 1933. — Steve Patterson Coll. Switcher 204 is shown (center) in 1946. — C. W. Witbeck. The 205 came from the RF&P and is shown at Elizabethton (opposite page) in 1950. — Lloyd Lewis Coll. Photographer C. W. Witbeck found the 205 at Johnson City (above) in 1946. — Ed Bond Coll.

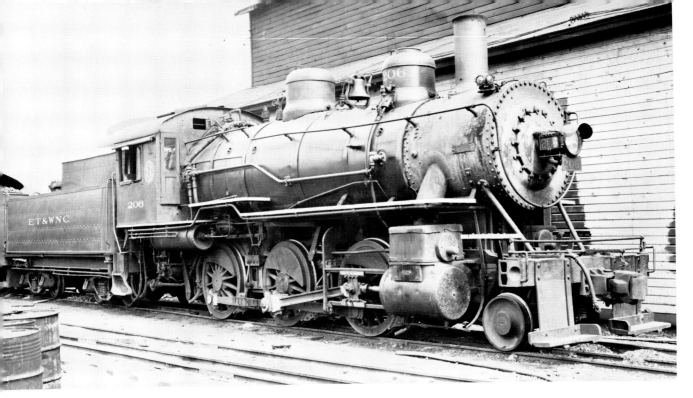

ET&WNC 206 came from the Illinois Central and is pictured (above) in 1948. — Tom Lawson, Jr. The 207 was former Southern 630 and is shown at Elizabethton in a 1956 view by Stanley Mailer. — Henry Bender Coll.

ET&WNC 208 (top) was a former Southern Railway engine. She is shown at Coal Chute in 1966. The 207 and 208 were traded to the Southern for a pair of former Central of Georgia RS-3 Alco units. Central of Georgia 108 (center) became ET&WNC 209, while the ET&WNC 210 is shown at Johnson City in 1973 (lower). — John E. Parker from Jim Wade Coll.

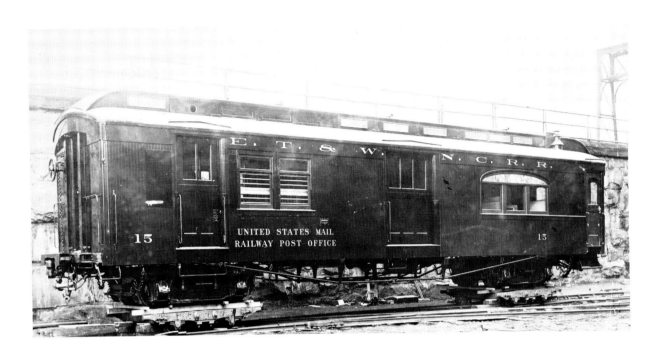

ET&WNC-LR PASSENGER CARS

NO.	TYPE	BUILDER	DATE	LENGTH	REMARKS
1	Combine		1880	40	Retired 1938
2	Coach		1880	40	Retired 1927
3	Coach		1882	40	Retired 1938
4	Coach		1883	38	Transferred to L.R. 1917, to ET&WNC 1941, sold.
5	Combine	2nd Hand		40	2nd Hand from Lancaster & Chester Ry. in 1907, to L.R. 1917, retired 1938.
6	Combine	2nd Hand		40	2nd Hand from Lancaster & Chester Ry. in 1907, retired 1938.
7	Coach	2nd Hand		38	2nd Hand from Lancaster & Chester Ry. in 1907, transferred to L.R. 1917, retired 1938.
8 (1st)	Coach	2nd Hand		42	2nd Hand from Lancaster & Chester Ry. in 1907, retired 1924.
8 (2nd)	Coach	ET&WNC	6/1924	43	Note 1.
9	Bag-Mail	2nd Hand		36	2nd Hand from Lancaster & Chester Ry. in 1907, retired 1938.
10 (1st)	Parlor	ET&WNC	c. 1902		"Ethel" Burned in Johnson City Coach Shed fire in 1907.
10 (2nd)	Parlor	Jackson & Sharp		40	"Azalea" Retired 1935. Note 1.
11	Excursion	ET&WNC	1911	33	Sold 1952 Shenandoah Central R.R. Sold 1955 Tweetsie R.R.
12	Excursion	ET&WNC	1911	33	Retired 1938.
13	Excursion	ET&WNC	1917	33	Retired 1938.
14	Excursion	ET&WNC	1917	33	Retired 1938.
15	Combine	AC&F-J&S	11/1917	40	Sold 1952 Shenandoah Central R.R. Sold 1955 Tweetsie R.R.
16	Coach	AC&F-J&S	1919	40	Note 1.

17	Coach	AC&F-J&S	1919	40	Note 1.
18	Bag-Mail	AC&F-J&S	1921	40	Linville River 18, transferred to ET&WNC 1941, retired.
19	Coach	AC&F-J&S	1921	40	Linville River 19. Note 1.
20	Coach	AC&F-J&S	1921	40	Linville River 20. Note 1.
21	Bag-Mail	ET&WNC	4/1923	43	Note 1.
22	Coach	Laconia		45	Purchased 11/1923 from General Equipment Co., Lynn, Mass. Formerly Boston, Revere Beach & Lynn. Body to Times Square Diner, Elk Park, N.C.
23	Coach	Laconia		45	Purchased 11/1923 from General Equipment Co., Lynn, Mass. Formerly Boston, Revere Beach & Lynn. Retired 1940. Body to Tweetsie Cafe, Newland, N.C.
24	Coach	Laconia		45	Purchased 11/1923 from General Equipment Co., Lynn, Mass. Formerly Boston, Revere Beach & Lynn. Retired 1945. Body to residence west of Newland, N.C., later moved to "Hillbilly World," Hampton, Tenn.
25	Coach	Laconia		45	Purchased 11/1923 from General Equipment Co., Lynn, Mass. Formerly Boston, Revere Beach & Lynn. Retired 1945.
26	Combine	2nd Hand		38	Note 2, Transferred to L.R. 1926. Note 1.
27	Coach	2nd Hand		38	Note 2, note 1.
					NOTE 1: Sold 1936 to Georgia Car & Locomotive Company for United Fruit Company service.
					NOTE 2: Original Twin Mountain & Potomac R.R., Keyser, W. Va. to West Virginia Tie & Lumber Co. (Rapidan R.R.), Orange, Virginia to ET&WNC/LR 1/1926.

ET&WNC 15 is shown (opposite) at the Jackson & Sharp plant in 1917. — Ed Bond Coll. Linville River coach 4 is pictured (below) at Johnson City, Tennessee in 1940. She was one of the original ET&WNC cars of the 1880's.

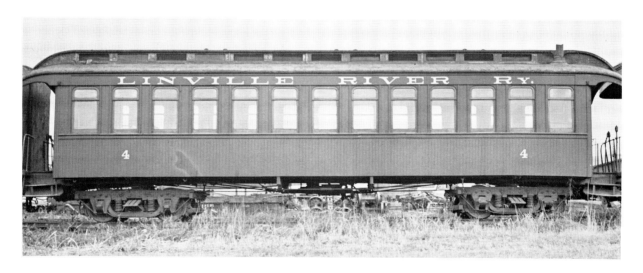

Linville River coach 4 (left) was built in 1883 for the ET&WNC and is pictured at Johnson City in 1941. Excursion car 11 was built in the company shops in 1911 and is still in existence. The car is shown at Elizabethton in 1950. — Lloyd Lewis Coll.

ET&WNC car 15 was unique in that it had compartments for mail, express and passengers. It is shown at Johnson City during the late 1930's. — Jim Bower Coll. Linville River car 18 was designed for use as an RPO-Baggage car on the all-vestibule train of 1921. The car was transferred to the ET&WNC in 1941.

 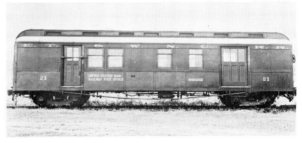

Linville River 20 was built by Jackson & Sharp in 1921 and sold to the United Fruit Company in 1936. She is shown (left) in 1935. — Lloyd Lewis Coll. ET&WNC Baggage 21 was an all steel car built in the company shops in 1923. She was top heavy and turned over at Love's Crossing soon after she was put in service. — George Allison.

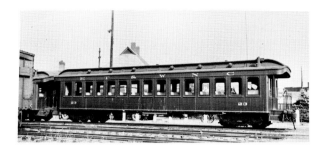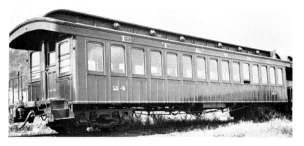

The ET&WNC purchased four coaches from the Boston, Revere Beach & Lynn in 1923. Car 23 is shown at Johnson City in 1938. — Hugh Boutell. Car 24 is shown in 1936. — R. W. Richardson.

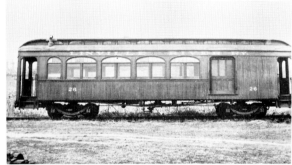

ET&WNC coach 25 is shown (left) at Johnson City. — C. W. Witbeck. Linville River combine 26 was purchased second hand and was soon sold to United Fruit Co. — George Allison.

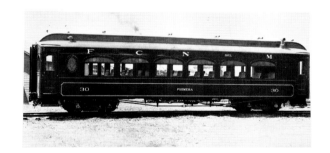

One of the ET&WNC-LR coaches is shown (left) lettered for its new owner, a United Fruit Company line. — Ed Bond Coll. Cars that were not sold for service in the banana republics ended their days as roadside cafes and summer cottages. Coach 23 served as the "Tweetsie Diner" near Newland, North Carolina. — Robert B. Adams.

ET&WNC hopper 1 was designed to carry iron ore from the Cranberry Mines to the Johnson City furnaces. It was one of the few cars that was not renumbered. It is shown at Johnson City, Tennessee on May 16, 1946 in a photograph by the late C. W. Witbeck. — Ed Bond Coll.

FREIGHT CAR ROSTER—1919-1927
NARROW GAUGE

NO.	TYPE	LENGTH	WIDTH	HEIGHT	CAP./WT.	NO. CARS	REMARKS
1- 4	Hopper	28'0"	7	4	40,000	4	
5- 40	Hopper	28'0"	7	4	50,000	36	
41- 80	Flat	32'0"	7		24,000	40	
81- 100	Gondola	28'0"	7	1'4"	24,000	20	
101- 120	Gondola	30'0"	7	3'0"	40,000	20	
121- 130	Box	32'0"	7	7'0"	40,000	10	
131- 145	Gondola	32'0"	7	3'0"	60,000	15	
146- 153	Box	32'0"	7	7'0"	60,000	8	
154- 165	Gondola	28'0"	7	1'4"	24,000	12	
166- 179	Side Dump	32'0"	7	3'0"	50,000	14	
180- 199	Flat	32'0"	7		50,000	20	
200, 202 205	Caboose	18'3"	7	9'9"		3	4-Wheel. Built ET&WNC Shops.
STANDARD GAUGE							
1000-1005	Gondola	34'0"	8'6"	2'6"	60,000	6	
1006-1007	Gondola	28'0"	8'6"	5'0"	60,000	2	

204

FREIGHT CAR ROSTER—1945

NO.	TYPE	LENGTH	WIDTH	HEIGHT	CAP/WT.	NO. CARS	REMARKS
1- 48	Hopper	28'0"	7	4'0"	40-50,000	28	McCord Trucks
101- 199	Gondola	36'0"	7	3'0"	40-60,000	37	McCord Trucks
241- 291	Flat	36'0"	7			6	
300- 378	Gondola	36'0"	7	3'0"	40-50,000		Totals included with 101-199 series.
400-445	Box	36'0"	7	7'0"	50,000	23	
600	Tank	32'0"			4606 gal	1	
605	Tank	32'0"			5000 gal	1	Cars 601-604 out of service.
700- 701	Stock	33'0"	7	7'0"	50,000	2	Last of 16 stock cars on roster in 1905. Not in service in 1945.
1018-1021	Tank	36'0"			7500 gal	4	
505, 506	Caboose	8-wheel				2	506 out of service. Blt. ET&WNC.

EQUIPMENT COLORS:
  Caboose—Boxcar Red/White Lettering
  Box—Boxcar Red/White Lettering
  Gondola—Black-White Lettering   Some: Boxcar Red/White Lettering
  Hopper—Black-White Lettering
  Flat—Black-White Lettering
  Tank—600 Series: Silver Tanks/Black Lettering/Black Underframes
       1000 Series: Black-White Lettering
  Passenger—Pullman Green Body/Boxcar Red Roof/White Lettering (Later Years)
       Pullman Green Body/Black Roof/Gold Leaf Lettering & Striping (Early)

The ET&WNC's clamshell crane is shown in a January 1942 photograph by G. P. Vance. She was a narrow gauge machine and is shown in front of the Johnson City enginehouse.
— Ed Bond Coll.

The boxcars of the Linville River were similar to those in use on the parent ET&WNC. Car 4 was photographed in the 1930's (left), while car 5 was found at Johnson City in 1942. — R. W. Richardson.

ET&WNC hopper cars changed little over the years. Car 12 is shown at Johnson City in 1946. — C. W. Witbeck. Hopper 48 was the last of the wooden hoppers to be built. — C. W. Witbeck from Ed Bond.

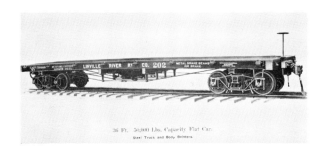

The Kilby Locomotive & Machine Co. built LR flat 202 (left). — Ed Bond Coll. Linville River 204, a convertible gondola is shown (right) at Johnson City in 1941.

ET&WNC flat 240 had racks for hauling acid wood to the Johnson City tannery. It is shown in a C. W. Witbeck photo on May 16, 1946. — Ed Bond Coll. Gondola 374 was photographed in 1938 at Johnson City.

ET&WNC narrow gauge tank cars came in two basic styles. The 601 (left) and 602 were silver with black lettering and underframes. The car is shown at Cranberry in 1941. The 1021 was photographed in 1938 and was painted black. — Hugh Boutell.

Caboose 505 served the ET&WNC narrow gauge lines until the final run. The car is shown at Johnson City in 1941. — G. P. Vance. ET&WNC 506 was out of service by 1938. Similar to the 505, she sported passenger trucks. — Hugh Boutell.

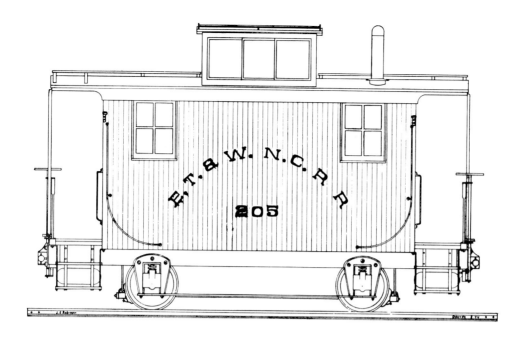

Drawing by John E. Robinson
Scale 1/4" = 1'0"

```
 1   2   3   4   5   6
                        SCALE
```

Caboose 205 was built in the ET&WNC shops in 1909 and later wrecked and destroyed at Cranberry, North Carolina. Cars 200 and 202 were similar and were 18'3" long. Car 205 is shown at Cranberry in 1910 with Conductor John Gorley, Brakeman Kyle Dennis, Finley Smith and James Livingston. — Cy Crumley.

E. T. & W. N. C. Caboose

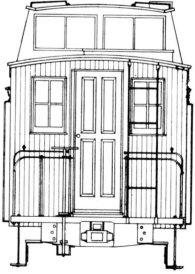

208

Quiet falls over the sleepy depot at Linville, North Carolina as the mixed train departs on an overcast September 20, 1936. The entire Blue Ridge Mountains are in the grip of the Great Depression and the daily passing of the Linville River train is about the only activity in many once active towns. — R. W. Richardson.

E. T. & W. N. C. — L. R. Stations

STATION	FACILITIES	MILE POST
Johnson City	Standpipe, shop, wye, dual gauge yards	0
Milligan	Siding	4
Watauga Point		6
Sycamore Schoals		8
Bemberg	Tank, wye, industrial sidings	9
Elizabethton	Tank, connection (Sou), ng enginehouse	10
Coal Chute (O'Brien)	(third rail stopped here after 1940) (n.g. engines brought std. g. coal cars) (here for n.g. engines coaling)	11
Valley Forge		12
	Gravity Tank	13.5
Hampton	House track	14
Pardee Point	(in the Gorge)	17
Blevins	Passing track	20
White Rock		22
	Gravity Tank	23
Crab Orchard (Crabtree)	Lumber loading track	24
Moreland Siding		25.5
Roan Mountain	House track (tank here in 1883)	26

Shell Creek	House track	28
Wilcox Bridge	(Not a station)	30
Greer Bridge	(Not a station—high fill—spur went to mine here) (2 miles up a cove)	30.5
Elk Park	House track, industrial loading tracks	32
Cranberry	Tank, wye, mine tracks, lumber loading, house tracks, engine and coach sheds	34
Cranberry Gap		36
Minneapolis	(switchback off mainline 5% **down** into town)	38
Buchannon	(note spelling)	39
Banjo Branch	(Gravity tank) (bridge and whistle post stands now)	39.5
Vale	(sidetrack to lumber mills)	40
Ram's Horn Curve		41
Newland	Tank, house track, passing track, commercial coal chute	42
Montezuma Junction	(Bull Scrape) highest P.O. in Eastern U.S. Elev. 3882	44
Love's Crossing		45
Pineola	Tank, wye, engine shed, lumber tracks	46
Junction Ledford's Siding	Doubling track for Linville Grade (this mile post still stands in Ledford's pasture)	45
Linville	Tank, house track	46
Linville Gap	Wye	50
Jestes Siding		52
Valley Creek		54
Aldridge Tank		54.5
Foscoe	Passing track, loading track	56
Shulls Mills	Lumber tracks, yard, connections with lumber railroads	58
Laurel	Tank	59.5
Danner's Siding		61
Hodges Gap	(doubling track)	64
Winkler's Siding	(connection made here with lbr road)	65
Boone	Wye, house and industrial tracks	66

Bibliography

DIARIES, LETTERS, NEWSPAPERS, UNPUBLISHED MATERIALS

DIARIES

Diary of Doctor Abram Jobe, Elizabethton, Tennessee, June 13, 1881,

Private Letters

A. Pardee to J. C. Hardin, October 29, 1878; June 20, 1879; April 3, 1880; April 20, 1880.

A. Pardee, Jr., to J. C. Hardin, June 22, 1875.

Baldwin Locomotive Works, Philadelphia, Pennsylvania, to J. S. Wise, June 20, 1882; June 19, 1882; December 78, 1880.

C. M. McGhee to A. Pardee, June 17, 1880.

Henry Small to A. Pardee, Jr., August 6, 1880.

J. C. Hardin to C. W. Russell, February 14, 1872.

J. C. Hardin to J. Roswell King, April 21, 1874.

J. C. Hardin to A. Pardee, March 9, 1877.

N. M. Taylor to J. C. Hardin, September 17, 1875.

N. M. Taylor to A. Pardee, Jr., April 24, 1879; September 20, 1876.

R. F. Hoke to J. C. Hardin, July 19, 1875.

R. F. Hoke to A. Pardee, March 5, 1879.

Vice-President, East Tennessee, Virginia, and Georgia and Memphis and Charleston Railroads, to A. Pardee, Jr., April 24, 1880.

R. T. Wilson to A. Pardee, Jr., February 20, 1880.

William Malone to J. C. Hardin, December 21, 1874.

Newspapers

The Asheville Citizen, May 14, 1957; May 24, 1957.

Asheville Citizen-Times, May 19, 1957.

The Charlotte News, May 24, 1957; August 12, 1957.

The Charlotte Observer, July 31, 1938; January 10, 1953; May 10, 1956; July 12, 1957.

The Comet (early Johnson City, Tennessee, paper), January 18, 1906.

Greensboro Daily News, May 21, 1956.

Hickory Daily Record, May 10, 1956; May 14, 1956; May 16, 1956; May 18, 1956; May 19, 1956; May 22, 1956.

Hudson, North Carolina Courier, various Cal Caldwell articles 1970-1973.

Johnson City (Tennessee) *Press-Chronicle,* September 17, 1950, May 20, 1957, May 21, 1957.

Lenoir News-Topic, May 21, 1956; July 11, 1957.

The Miami Herald, June, 8, 1957.

The News and Observer of Raleigh, May 18, 1940; July 28, 1957.

Sullivan County News, (Blountville, Tennessee), March 15, 1951.

Watauga Democrat (Boone, North Carolina), January, 1918 — December, 1919.

Watauga Democrat (Boone, North Carolina), January, 1940 — December, 1941.

Watauga Democrat (Boone, North Carolina), January, 1950 — December, 1950.

Watauga Democrat (Boone, North Carolina), January, 1956 — December, 1957.

Unpublished Materials

Bowlick, C. A. "A Study of the Cranberry Ore Belt." Unpublished Master's thesis, Appalachian State Teachers College, Boone, 1955.

English, William Garvel, Jr. "The ET&WNC Transporation Company or the Evolution of Transport Facilities Within a Company." Unpublished Master's thesis, the University of Tennessee, Knoxville, 1955.

Epps, J. H. Jr. "A Resume of the Minutes of the ET&WNC Company." Johnson City: ET&WNC Transportation Company, 1951. (Typed.)

Hyder, J. H. "Estimate of Quantities and Cost." Johnson City: ET&WNC Railroda Company, 1880. (Written by Hand.)

Ward, Francis E. "Historical Study of E.T.&W.N.C. R.R.." Master's thesis, Appalachian State Teachers College, Boone, 1957.

Additional Materials

Copy of Authority of Sale of the ET&WNC Railroad for J. C. Hardin, dated December 28, 1874.

Certification of Appointment of George W. Hardin as Executor in the Last Will and Testment of J. C. Hardin, deceased. Under the Seal of Washington County, Tennessee, dated November 6, 1905.

File Containing Freight Bills and General Accounts of the ET&WNC Railroad Company 1881-1907.

Contract of the ET&WNC Railroad Company for Work Dealing with Grading and Masonry. Members of Contract: Joseph H. Lofrode and Francis H. Saylor. Dated August 26, 1880. Also Contract dated October 2, 1880, members of same party but Concerning Truss Bridges.

Specification Number 1417 of Baldwin Locomotive Works of the Burnham, Parry, Williams and Company. Dated June 19, 1882.

Agreement Between Western Union Telegraph Company and the ET&WNC Railroad Company. Dated August 30, 1882.

Mortgages of Deed of Trust of the ET&WNC Railroad Company to the Guarantee Trust and Safe Deposit Company of Philadelphia. Dated February 1, 1881.

Philadelphia Stock Exchange. Securities Listed. Johnson City, Tennessee. Dated June 2, 1906.

Abstract of Acts of Tennessee. *Act to Amend the Act entitled "An Act to Incorporate the Tennessee and Pacific Railroad Company;" and for other purposes.* Nashville: Acts 1867-68, Chapter LXXVIII. Passed January 25, 1868.

Abstract of Acts of Tenness. *Act to Amend the Act entitled "An Act to Incorporate the Tennessee and Pacific Railroad Company; and for other purposes.* Nashville: Acts 1868-70, Chapter VI. Passed December 16, 1868.

Copy of Interstate Commerce Finance Docket Number 16954. *East Tennessee and Western North Carolina Railroad Company Abandoment.* Washington: Government Printing Office, 1950. Decided September 6, 1950.

Copy of Interstate Commerce Commission Finance Docket Number 13029. *Lin-ville River Railway Company Abandonment.* Washington: Government Printing Office, 1941. Decided March 22, 1941.

Copy of Interstate Commerce Commission Finance Docket Number 12947. *East Tennessee and Western North Carolina Railroad Company Et Al. Control* Washington: Government Printing Office, 1940. Decided September 12, 1940.

North Carolina News Bureau. *Train of Yesterday.* Raleigh: Department of Conservation and Development, undated.

PERIODICALS

Alexander, Jack. "Tweetsie's Last Trip," *Trains,* XI No. 3 (January 1951), p. 24ff.

Beebe, Lucius. "All Aboard for the Old West," *This Week Magazine,* May 25, 1958. p. 14ff.

Finelines, Edited by Robert Brown, Los Gatos, California, September, 1971 (Plan of ET&WNC No. 7)

"Going, Going, Not Yet Gone," *The Saturday Evening Post,* Vol. 214 No. 43 (April 25, 1942), p. 20ff.

Holden, Bill. "The Onliest Train," *The Nashivlle Tennessean Magazine,* September 12, 1948, p. 5ff.

Maxwell, Henry V., "Developing Iron & Timber," Manufacturers Record, June 5, 1913, page 71 (Vol LXIII, Number 22)

The MacRae Lumber Company operated this narrow gauge Shay (Lima 2131-1909) as well as a small Climax out of their Linville mill. The Shay was photographed by L.L. Norton on August 15, 1937. — Tom Lawson, Jr. Col.

Model Railroader, Kalmbach Publishing Company, Milwaukee, Wisconsin, December, 1968 (Plan of ET&WNC No. 5)

Narrow Gauge News, Narrow Gauge Meseum, Alamosa, Colorado, Edited by R. W. Richardson, Vol. 1, No. 3, October, 1949.

Railroad Magazine, New York: The following issues: October 1932; November 1933; July 1942; August 1943; January 1951; February 1957; February 1961; August 1966.

Reilly, Richard L. (ed.). "Trucks Used to Haul Train," *Highway Highlights,* June, 1957, p. 6ff.

Sharpe, Bill (pub.). "Tweetsie," *The State,* XXV (June, 1957), p. 28.

Trains Magazine, Kalmbach Publishing Company, Milwaukee, Wisconsin. "Tweetsie Narrow Gauge," December 1942, p. 18; Also: July 1951; November 1952; March 1953; October 1954; July 1955; March 1955, February 1959; July 1960.

Wohl, Harry D. "A Train Called 'Tweetsie' Shipped . . . by Truck!," *American Cartegemen,* IV (August, 1957), p. 6ff.

D. PAPERS

Association of American Railroads. *Railroad.* Washington: The Association, undated.

Collected Papers of D. B. Marion, Johnson City, Tennessee. A Collection of Unpublished Materials of the ET&WNC Transportation Company.

ET&WNC Motor Car 1 provided transportation for track crews and was photographed at Johnson City in 1947. — Jim Bower Coll.

Collected Papers of Edwin S. Dougherty, Boone, North Carolina. A Collection of Unpublished Materials of I.C.C. Finance Docket 13029 and Other Materials.

Whisman, W. W. *Souvenir Programme, 85th Year of Service.* Johnson City: East Tennessee and Western North Carolina Transportation Company, 1951.

Interstate Commerce Commission: Washington, D.C.
ICC Finance Docket No. 16954, 1950.
ICC Finance Docket No. 13029, 1941.
ICC Finance Docket No. 129478, 1940.

An ET&WNC Railroad Six Per Cent First Mortgage Loan. Due Date November 1, 1905

Joint and Local Tariff File of the ET&WNC Railroad Company. Property of D.B. Marion, Johnson City, Tennessee.

Time Table Number 78 of Linville River Railroad Company.

Time Table Number 4 of the ET&WNC Railroad Company. October 15, 1883.

Time Table Numbers 1, 26, 121, 122, 123, 124, 126.

BOOKS

Arthur, John P., *History of Watauga County,* Richmond: Everett Waddy Company, 1915.

Beebe, Lucius, *Mixed Train Daily, New York*: E. P. Dutton and Company, Inc., 1947.

Brown, Cecil Kenneth, *A State Movement in Railroad Development,* Chapel Hill: The University of North Carolina Press, 1928.

Cooper, Horton, *History of Avery County,* Asheville: North Carolina, Biltmore Press, 1964 (pp. 44-45).

Dugger, Shepherd M., *The War Trails of the Blue Ridge,* Charlotte: Observer Printing House, 1932.

Iron Manufactures Guide, 1859, Chapel Hill: University of North Carolina Library Collections.

Official Railway Equipment Register, New York: Railway Equipment & Publication Co., 1902-1945

Poor, Henry V., *Poor's Manual of Railroads,* New York: Henry V. Poor, 1867-1920 (Colorado Railroad Museum Archives).

Reid, Harold, *Extra South,* Susquehanna, Pa.: Starrucca Publications, 1964.

Richardson, Helen R. (Ed.), *Railroads in Defense and War,* Washington: Bureau of Railway Economics Library, 1953.

Robertson, Archie, *Slow Train to Yesterday,* New York: Somerset Books, Inc., 1945.

Scheer, Julian and Black, Elizabeth, *Tweetsie: The Blue Ridge Stemwinder,* Charlotte: Heritage House, 1958.

Southern Railroads, TRAINS Album of Kalmbach Publishing Company, Milwaukee, Wisconsin.

Stover, John F., *The Railroads of the South* 1865–1900, Chapel Hill: The University of North Carolina Press, 1955.

Warner, Ezra J., *General in Gray, Lives of the Confederate Commanders,* Baton Rouge: L.S.U. Press, 1959.

Whitener, Daniel J., *History of Watauga County,* Kingsport: Franklin Printing Company, 1949.

Wigginton, Eliot, *The Foxfire Book,* (Ed). New York: Doubleday & Company, 1972.

PUBLICATIONS OF THE GOVERNMENT, SOCIETIES, AND OTHER ORGANIZATIONS

United States Department of Agriculture. *Report on an Examination of a Forest Tract in Western North Carolina,* Bulletin Number 60. Washington: Government Printing Office, 1905.

Abstract of Acts of Tennessee. *Act to Allow the Commissioners of the East Tennessee and Virginia Rail Road Company further time to carry into effect the provisions of said act.* Nashville: Acts 1849-50, 1851-52, Chapter XI. Passed November 6, 1849.

Abstract of Acts of Tennessee. *Act to establish a system of Internal Improvements in this State.* Nashville: Acts 1849-50, 1851-52, Chapter CLI. Passed February 11, 1852.

Abstract of Acts Tennessee. *Act to Incorporate the Tennessee Pacific Rail Road Company, and for other purposes.* Nashville: Acts 1865-66, Chapter LXXXVIII. Passed May 24, 1866.

Abstract of Acts of Tennessee. *Act to Amend an Act passed January* 18, 1866, *entitled "An Act to establish a system of Internal Improvement,"* Passed February 11, 1852. Nashville: Acts 1866-67, Chapter XII, Passed December 10, 1866.

Abstract of Acts of Tenness. *Act to Authorize the issue of Bonds by the City of Nashville; and for other purposes.* Nashville: Acts 1867-68, Chapter XXVII. Passed December 17, 1867.

Abstract of Acts of Tennessee. *Act to Amend the Charter of the Atlantic, Tennessee and Ohio Railroad Company; and for other purposes.* Nashville: Acts 1867-68, Chapter XXXIV. Passed December 14, 1867.

Abstract of Acts of Tennessee. *Act to give the County of Carter the right to take stock in the East Tennessee and Western North Carolina Railroad so amended to be goverened by rules, regulations, and restrictions as in the case of the County of Johnson.* Nashville: Acts 1867-68, Section Twenty, Chapter LIX. Passed February 17, 1868.

Index

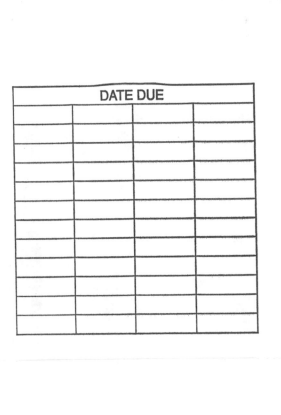

DATE DUE
